anyone
can tell a
Bible Story

anyone can tell a Bible Story

Bob Hartman

MONARCH
BOOKS

Oxford, UK & Grand Rapids, Michigan, USA

This edition first published in the UK in 2011 by Monarch Books
(a publishing imprint of Lion Hudson plc)
Wilkinson House, Jordan Hill Road, Oxford OX2 8DR, England
Tel: +44 (0)1865 302750 Fax: +44 (0)1865 302757
Email: monarch@lionhudson.com
www.lionhudson.com

ISBN 978 0 85721 007 4

An earlier edition of this book, *Anyone Can Tell a Story*, was published in 2002 by Lion Children's, an imprint of Lion Hudson plc.

Distributed by:
UK: Marston Book Services, PO Box 269, Abingdon, Oxon, OX14 4YN
USA: Kregel Publications, PO Box 2607, Grand Rapids, Michigan 49501

The text paper used in this book has been made from wood independently certified as having come from sustainable forests.

British Library Cataloguing Data
A catalogue record for this book is available from the British Library.

Printed and bound in Malta by Gutenberg Press

FOR EVERYONE AT OPEN THE BOOK

acknowledgments

A big thanks to my brother Tim, without whom this book would not have been possible.

Thanks to my Grandma Brosi, as well, without whom I would have not been possible. And whose offbeat Sunday school classes sparked off the storyteller in me.

Thanks also to everyone at Monarch – Tony, Roger, Jenny and Simon – for your skill, patience and encouragement. Another book! Another shirt!

Contents

List of Stories

Preface

Several years ago, I wrote a book called *Anyone Can Tell a Story*. It was written, as the title suggests, for anyone who wanted to tell *any* kind of story.

Since I wrote that book, seven or eight years ago, I have learned a lot more about the art of storytelling. During that time, as well as retelling many old favourites, I have also rewritten and retold a lot more stories, most of them from the Bible. So it makes sense, I think, to pass on what I have learned, and also to do it in the context of biblical storytelling, since that is the area in which I have gained the most experience.

As a result, some of the content of *this* book has been carried over from the previous one (no point in re-inventing the wheel!). But a lot of it is new, and reflects my experience and discoveries in those intervening years.

Anyone Can Tell a Bible Story is broken up into five chapters. The first gives a history of my "storytelling life". You will see that I had no formal training in the art; I just picked it up as I went along, learning by trial and error. Since that is the case, I think you may find it helpful to trace that progress and, I hope, learn something from my journey, as well.

The next chapter is all about my philosophy of storytelling. Don't be afraid. I use the term "philosophy" loosely. However, I think that if you're going to do something well, it helps to know why you're doing what you do – the theory needs to come before the "nuts and bolts". And because I believe that storytelling works largely because it is relational in nature, I outline the four relationships that are at the heart of biblical storytelling.

In the following chapter, I look at how stories "work", and show how I take a Bible story apart and then put it back together as a retelling. I will also explain how this process will help you discover the elements of a story that will make it "shine" for you – and help you retell it yourself with passion and enthusiasm.

In the fourth chapter, I set out the (mostly) traditional tips and techniques that storytellers use to engage their audiences and make them a part of the story. It's essentially the process of "de-audience-ification"!

Finally, I have included a chapter on reading the Bible in public, largely because I think there is a crying need for it (I have certainly shed the odd tear during that part of the service). Much of what makes good biblical storytelling work can also be applied to the public reading of the Bible.

At the end of each of the first four chapters (and at the end of some sections within them), you will find a set of stories which I have selected to illustrate the key points of that chapter. These include brand new stories and some old ones – mostly from books that are now out of print. Before each story, I explain how it fits into the chapter and suggest some "telling tips" that you can use to bring that story to life.

I have tried to make this book as user-friendly as possible, and I hope that it works for you. Even more, I hope that it helps you to become a better storyteller. As I say at the start of every workshop I lead, I don't have all the answers and no two storytellers are alike. All I can do is to share what has worked for me. If it is of some help to you, as well, then this book will have achieved its purpose.

Introduction

When we were kids, my brothers and I used to take turns spending the weekend with our Grandma Brosi. As is often the case with grandparents, she would let us do all the things that our mum and dad wouldn't. This included consuming large quantities of sweets, fizzy drinks and sugared cereals, and, best of all, staying up well past our bedtime on a Saturday night. Usually, that was seven-thirty or eight o'clock. Grandma, however, would always let us stay up and watch *Chiller Theater*, which didn't even start until the late-night news had finished at eleven!

Chiller Theater was a Pittsburgh institution. It was hosted by the local TV weatherman, dressed up like Dracula, and featured both some of the best and some of the cheesiest black-and-white horror films. We'd sit there in the dark, chewing on sweets, gulping down Cokes and scaring ourselves silly before crawling reluctantly into bed.

The following morning, Grandma Brosi would teach our Sunday school class – and, somehow, all that creepy stuff from the night before would find its way into the Bible stories that she told! Battles were brilliant! Evil kings were really nasty! And I can't even begin to describe the way in which she depicted the demise of wicked Queen Jezebel! Or recounted how Queen Athalia ascended to the throne of Judah by murdering all but one of her grandchildren, step by gory step! What I can say, though, is that those stories stuck. I can remember, to this day, how she told us about the tenth Egyptian plague – the death of the firstborn – and then looked around the room at those of us who were the oldest in our families, and solemnly said, "That would be you, Sammy. And you, Chucky. And," (pointing her bony finger in my direction) "you, Bobby, too!"

Biblical storytelling can do one of two things. It can excite and inspire and create a thirst for more. Or it can bore and embarrass and leave a group with a sad sense of "so what?" And that's an important difference if you believe, as I do, that those stories contain something essential about who we are and who God is. It's that collision, I think – my story and God's story – that leads to faith, and also has been instrumental in my development as a storyteller, in general, and more particularly, as someone who is committed to telling Bible stories with as much passion and wit and creativity as I can muster. So I'll start off by telling you my story. A storyteller's story. But before that, I thought you might like to read some examples of the kinds of stories my Grandma liked to tell.

Athalia – The Wicked Granny's Tale

As this book started with my Grandma Brosi and her unique approach to biblical storytelling, I thought it might be nice to offer some examples of the kind of stories that my grandma told me.

This is an obscure story, to be sure, from 2 Chronicles 22–23. In fact, when I mention it in churches, I often get blank stares. But it's one that my grandma told a lot, which is strange in a way, since it's all about a grandmother who murders her grandchildren so she can become Queen of Judah! Frankly, I'm just happy that I never had anything Grandma wanted. The story was originally in *More Bible Baddies*, a collection which is now out of print.

Telling tips: *Just enter into the spirit of the thing – that's what Grandma would have done – a mad smile on her face as Athalia's wickedness is revealed, and an even madder one at her comeuppance.*

Sweet and gentle. Wise and kind. Kitchens rich with the smell of fresh-baked treats. That's what grannies are like!

But Athalia was not your typical granny.

She was cruel and ambitious, deceitful and sly. And she had never baked a biscuit in her life! Evil plots were her speciality, and she cooked one up the moment she heard that her son, the king, was dead.

She gathered her guards around her. She whispered the recipe in their ears. And even though they were used to violence and to war, they could not hide the horror in their eyes.

"Yes, I know they're my grandsons," Athalia sneered. "But I want you to kill them, so that I, and I alone, will inherit the throne!"

Athalia was not your typical granny. And she hadn't been much of a mother either. So perhaps that is why her daughter, Jehosheba, was not surprised when she peeped into the hallway and saw soldiers marching, swords drawn, towards the nursery door.

Jehosheba had a choice. She could rush to the nursery and throw herself in front of her little nephews – and be killed along with them, more likely than not. Or she could creep back into the room from which she'd come, and try to save the king's youngest son – the baby she'd been playing with when she'd heard the soldiers pass.

The cries from the nursery answered her question. She was already too late, and she cursed the palace guards for their speed and efficiency. Speed was what she needed, as well, for she could hear the guards' voices coming her way.

"Did we get them all?"

"We'd better get them all?"

"The queen will have our heads if we've missed one."

And so they burst into each room, one by one, down the long palace hall, and Jehosheba had time – barely enough time – to wrap her hand round the baby's mouth and duck into a cupboard.

"Don't cry," she prayed, as the soldiers grunted and shuffled around the room. "Please don't cry."

"No one here," someone said at last. But Jehosheba stayed in that cupboard, as still as a statue, long after they had left the room. Then she wrapped up the baby in an old blanket and bundled him off to her home in the temple precincts.

Athalia stared sternly at her soldiers.

"So you killed them? Every last one?" she asked.

"Every last one," they grunted back. And Athalia's stare turned into an evil grin.

"Then tell me about it," she ordered. "And don't leave out one tiny detail."

When the guards had finished their story, Athalia sent them out of the room, and then she tossed back her head and cackled.

"At last. At last! AT LAST! Queen of Judah. Mother of the nation. That has a nice ring to it. And my parents... my parents would be so proud!"

Across the temple precincts, Jehosheba's husband, Jehoiada, however, had a very different reaction.

"Well, what did you expect?" he fumed, when Jehosheba told him about the murder of their nephews. "With a father like Ahab and a mother like Jezebel... well, the apple doesn't fall far from the tree!"

"But I'm HER daughter!" Jehosheba protested. "You don't mean to say..."

"No. NO!" Jehoiada assured his wife, as he wrapped his arms around her. "I didn't mean that at all. You are a wonderful mother – a good woman who knows the One True God. And because of your love and courage little Joash, here, is still alive."

"The true ruler of Judah," Jehosheba added. "If only the people knew. You're the high priest. Perhaps you could tell them..."

"Even if they knew, they would do nothing," Jehoiada sighed. "Athalia is much too powerful, and they are still entranced by the false gods she worships. No, we must wait – wait until they have seen through her evil ways. And then, and only then, dare we show this little fellow to them. Meanwhile, we shall hide him here, in the high priest's quarters, in the temple of the One True God. For this is the last place your wicked mother will want to visit."

One year passed. And while little Joash learned to crawl and then to walk, his evil grandmother was busy murdering anyone who dared to take a step against her.

Two years passed. And as Joash spoke his first words and toddled around the temple, Athalia sang the praises of the false god Baal and offered him the blood of human sacrifice.

Three years, four years, five years passed. And as Joash grew into a little boy, the people of Judah grew tired of Athalia's evil ways.

Six years passed, then seven. And when Joash was finally old enough to understand who he was, Jehoiada decided that the time had come to tell the nation, as well.

"We must be very careful," he explained to his wife. "The palace guards are finally on our side, but your mother still has some support among the people. We mustn't show our hand too soon."

"So how will you do it?" Jehosheba asked.

"On the sabbath, it is the usual custom for two thirds of the palace guard to stay at the temple while the others return to the palace to protect the queen. Tomorrow, however, the bodyguards will leave as expected, but they will not go to the palace. Instead they will return to the temple by another route and help to protect young Joash, should anything happen."

"Ah!" Jehosheba smiled. "So Joash will be surrounded by the entire palace guard – while my mother will be left with no soldiers to do her bidding!"

"Exactly!" Jehoiada grinned back.

When the sabbath came, the people gathered in the temple, as usual, to worship the One True God. But there was nothing usual about what happened at the end of the service. Jehoiada, the high priest, led a little boy out in front of the crowd. Then he placed a crown on that little boy's head. And while the palace guard gathered round the child, the high priest shouted:

"Behold, people of Judah! Behold your true king! Behold Joash, son of Ahaziah!"

All was silent for a moment and then someone cheered. Someone else joined in and soon the cheering filled the temple and echoed from there to the palace, where Athalia was waiting, wondering what had happened to her guards.

She was old and frail now, but as wicked and as stubborn as ever!

"What's going on? What's all the noise about?" she muttered as she hobbled out of the palace and across to the temple.

"Out of my way! Get out of my way!" she ordered. And the crowd parted before her. And that's when something caught her eye – a glint, a gleaming from the little king's crown.

"What's the meaning of this?" she glared. "This looks like treason to me!"

"Not treason, Athalia," said the high priest. "But the true king of Judah restored to his rightful throne – Joash, your grandson!"

"My grandson?" Athalia shuddered. "But I thought... I mean... my soldiers... they told me..."

"That they had murdered them all?" asked Jehoiada. "Is that what you meant to say? Well, in their haste to fulfil your wicked ambition, they missed one – the one who stands before you now. The true king of Judah!"

"Treason!" shouted the old woman again, but her words were stifled by the palace guard that quickly surrounded her.

"Where are we going? What are you doing?" she demanded to know as they led her away. "I'm an old woman – a grandmother – don't push me!"

"Don't worry, granny," one of the guards whispered in her ear. "This won't take long. Remember what you had us do to your grandsons all those years ago? Well we're going to do the same thing to you now!"

Athalia shrieked, but only the guards heard her final cry, for the crowds were still cheering – cheering for Athalia's grandson and for the end of her wicked reign.

Ahab and Jezebel – The Rotten Ruler's Tale

Here's another Scary Matriarch Special. And it will come as no surprise that it's related to the previous story. That's right, Jezebel was Athalia's mum! Apples. Falling. Trees.

As you will see, I have tried to explore the humour in this tale (or perhaps, in memory of Grandma, simply invented it). But it does strike me that Ahab's determination to match the evil of his wife is consistent with what the Bible has to say about her leading him astray. This originally came from *More Bible Baddies*, as well.

Telling tips: *This story needs to be told with your tongue firmly planted in your cheek, and a hint of that mad smile again wouldn't do any harm, either.*

King Ahab wanted to be wicked. He wanted it in the worst kind of way! But he lacked the courage. And he lacked the imagination. And worst of all, he lacked the will – the "killer instinct" that true wickedness demands.

His queen, Jezebel, however, lacked nothing. She was, without question, the most wicked woman he had ever met. And this just made things worse. For, given her expertise at evil, her artistic flair for foul play, he could never hope to impress her with any wickedness of his own.

She sensed this, of course (even the most wicked have their compassionate side), and tried her best to cheer him up.

"Who's the wicked one, then?" she would ask playfully over breakfast.

And Ahab would blush and lower his eyes and answer coyly, "You don't mean me, do you, darling?"

"Of course I do!" she would coo. "Who betrayed his own people? Who put my god, Baal, in place of Yahweh the god of Israel? Who murdered Yahweh's prophets? And who chased his true believers into hiding? It was you, my dear – that's who. Wicked King Ahab!"

"Well, I couldn't have done it alone," he would mutter in a humble, "aw-shucks" sort of way. "I had a wonderfully wicked wife to help me."

"Nonsense!" Jezebel would blush in return. "You're quite wonderfully wicked all on your own!"

Then the conversation would turn to the weather (dry, *always* dry), or to the state of the economy (failing crops, starving cattle), and ultimately to that pesky prophet, Elijah, who had somehow managed to stop the rains from falling.

"If I ever get hold of him," Ahab would rant, "I'll murder him – right there on the spot!"

"I'll do more than that!" Jezebel would counter. "I'll torture him – slowly – and stand there and laugh as he dies!"

"I'll rip off his fingers!" Ahab would return.

"I'll tear out his hair!" Jezebel would shriek.

And on and on it would go, until the two of them would collapse in fits of evil laughter, and then set off to do their day's worth of evil deeds. It was, on the whole, a sick sort of relationship. But it seemed to work.

One morning, however, King Ahab failed to appear at the breakfast table. And when Jezebel found him – on his bed, in his room – he had a woefully *un*wicked expression on his face.

"What's the matter, dear?" Jezebel chirped. "Run out of prophets to kill?"

"No," Ahab sighed. "Something much worse than that. It's the vineyard, next door."

"Naboth's vineyard?" queried Jezebel. "What could possibly be the problem with Naboth's vineyard?"

"It's in the way!" Ahab moaned. "That's the problem! My little garden is much too small. I want to put in some cabbages next year. And some sprouts. And two more rows of those little potatoes you like so well. But his stupid vineyard is right smack up against the property line. I've offered to buy it. I'd give him more than what it's worth. But the selfish so-and-so refuses to sell! So what can I do?"

Jezebel tried hard to hide her disappointment. There were plenty of things that Ahab could do. He was king, after all! And a wicked king (or a wicked wannabe), as well. The answer was obvious. But would telling him, straight up, snuff out the spark of true villainy she had worked so hard to ignite? Would it fracture his already brittle evil self-esteem? In the end, she decided that a simple demonstration would be the clearest (and, surely, the most compassionate) response of all.

"Leave it to me," she said quietly. Then she turned the conversation to the weather.

And, later that day, while Ahab was out digging in the garden, Jezebel sneaked into his office and picked up his pen. She wrote letters to all the elders and noblemen in Naboth's home town. She forged Ahab's signature (she'd had plenty of practice – so it was perfect!). And she stamped each letter with Ahab's special seal!

My dear friend and servant, (each letter began)

I have a favour to ask of you. Would you proclaim a day of fasting – a special, holy day – in your town? Would you be so kind as to invite my neighbour, Naboth, to this event (he has a lovely vineyard, don't you think)? Would you give him the most prominent seat at the event – some place where everyone can see him? And then would you hire two villains (I have names and references if it would be helpful) and ask them to stand up in the middle of the ceremony and accuse Naboth of some heinous crime? Blasphemy against his god, perhaps. And disloyalty to the king. And then, and I hope this is not asking too much, would you drag Naboth from that place and stone him to death?

Thanks very much for your consideration. I do hope that this will not be too much of an inconvenience. As always, my concern is for your continued health and well-being, which will be assured by your prompt response to this request.

Regards.

Ahab, King of Israel

Jezebel cackled and clapped her hands and hopped up and down in her seat. There was a joy to pure evil that never failed to delight her. Naboth would die (she had never liked him as a neighbour anyway!) Ahab would get his vineyard, and the local noblemen would be convinced, once and for all, of her husband's utter and total depravity. She couldn't wait to see the look on his face.

Her wait lasted only a few days. Ahab appeared at breakfast, one morning – a changed man.

"I'll have two eggs for breakfast, this morning," he grinned. "And – why not, by Baal! – a few rashers of bacon, as well!"

"So what's got into you?" asked Jezebel innocently.

"Haven't you heard, my dear?" Ahab beamed. "Naboth is dead. His widow wants to sell. And now, at last, his vineyard is mine!"

"How wonderful!" said the queen. "So tell me – how did poor Naboth die?"

"It was most unusual," Ahab mumbled through a mouthful of egg. "Blasphemy. Treason. Not very neighbourly, if you ask me. But then the rumour is that the charges were trumped-up. As if…" And here the king's chewing became more deliberate. "As if someone truly wicked had it in for him." And here he stared at his queen.

Jezebel could contain herself no longer. She blushed and she nodded, like a schoolgirl caught with a love note.

"Yes, my darling, I was the one who arranged it. I thought, at first, that it might be better to leave it to you – wicked man that you are. But you were so miserable! And, in the end, I just wanted to see you happy again."

Ahab held up his hand. "Enough," he said, solemnly. There were tears in his eyes, and little yellowy bits of egg on his trembling lips. "I have been blessed with the most exquisitely evil wife in the whole world. What more, I ask, could a malevolent monarch want?"

And then he gave Jezebel a big, sloppy, eggy kiss. It was, on the whole, a disgusting thing. But it seemed to work for them.

Ahab's celebration, however, was short-lived. For as he strolled through his new vineyard later that day, he was surprised by an unexpected guest.

"Elijah!" Ahab cried. "What are you doing here?"

The king's voice was shaking. Shaking with anger, as he remembered the threats he had shared with his wife. And shaking with fear, as well – for this was the man who had stopped the rain.

"I have a message for you from my God," Elijah solemnly replied. "The God who sent a drought upon this land. The God who defeated the prophets of Baal. The God who was once your God too.

"'You have sold yourself to evil,' says the Lord. 'And so, on the very spot where the dogs lapped up the blood of Naboth, they shall lap up your blood too.'"

Ahab's shaking was all fear now. "Naboth… no… you don't understand," he tried to explain. "Jezebel… it was all her doing."

"'And as for your wife, Jezebel,'" the prophecy continued, "'the dogs will do even more. They will chew her to pieces and leave so little behind that even her dearest friends will not be able to recognize her!'"

Ahab wanted to be wicked. He really did. He wanted to turn his evil threats into reality. He wanted to rip off Elijah's fingers and tear out Elijah's hair and torture Elijah and murder him. But it's hard to be wicked – really hard – when what you actually feel like doing is wetting your pants!

Ahab was scared – more scared than he had ever been in his whole sorry life. So he ran from the vineyard and hid in his room and wept and wailed and hoped that Jezebel wouldn't notice.

The noise was hard to miss, however, and Jezebel was humiliated by her husband's behaviour – a feeling that turned to disgust when he told her his battle plans over breakfast, one morning.

"It looks like we have to fight the Syrians," he explained, as he lifted a dripping spoonful of porridge to his mouth. "And the prophets have told me that I will die in the battle."

"Not Elijah, again!" Jezebel moaned. "If I hear the story about the dogs one more time…"

"No, no! Not just Elijah," Ahab interrupted. "But Micaiah, as well – a prophet from Judah!" And Ahab dropped the spoon back into the bowl. "But here's the thing," he went on. "I think I have outsmarted them. And it's a plan so devious that I am sure you will approve. When I go into battle, tomorrow, I will not be dressed as Ahab, king of Israel. I will wear a disguise! The Syrians will try to kill some other poor fool and I shall escape unharmed!"

Jezebel was appalled. And so upset that she thought she would lose her breakfast, right then and there. After all her work, all her training, all her coaxing and encouraging and example setting, had it come down to this? Her husband was not evil. Her husband was not wicked. He was a nasty little man, at best. And a coward, to boot!

"All right, my dear," she said, very quietly. "Whatever you think is best." But inwardly she hoped that she would never have to look at that face again.

Her wish came true, of course. Ahab disguised himself, just as he said he would. But a stray arrow struck him, anyway. He bled to death in his chariot, and when his servants washed the chariot down, they did so at the same spot where Naboth had died. So just as Elijah had predicted, the dogs lapped up Ahab's blood.

A civil war broke out in Israel. The king's heirs and commanders fought for control of the country, and in the end it was a man named Jehu who was victorious. He rode to Jezebel's house one morning, even before she had had breakfast.

She knew he was coming. It was inevitable. So she put on her best clothes and make-up. "He's a ruthless man," she thought. "Perhaps I can win him over and make him more ruthless still."

But Jehu was quite ruthless enough already. When he saw her in the window, he called out to her servants and demanded that any who were loyal to him should seize her and throw her out of the window to the ground.

There were plenty of volunteers, and while Jehu went into the house and had something to eat, the dogs breakfasted on the body of the dead queen.

"Someone had better bury that woman," he said to one of his servants. But when the servant went out in the street, there was nothing left to do. Elijah's prophecy had come true again – there was nothing left of Jezebel but her skull and her feet and the palms of her hands!

Chapter 1
a Storyteller's Story

I can't remember exactly when it began.

Was it that time under the blankets, late into the night, with the dimming torch and the second-hand copy of *The Call of the Wild*?

Was it the Junior Boys' Sunday school class and my grandma's grizzly account of Ehud's left-handed execution of evil King Eglon?

Or was it those prizes I received on the last day of school, the year I turned eight: the plastic dinosaur that I lost before the summer ended and the book about the magic umbrella that my mother still reads to her grandchildren?

I can't remember exactly when it started. It just seems that I have always loved stories. And I suppose that is why I became a storyteller. It's the essential requirement, surely!

You see, I can't really claim to be an expert in the field of storytelling – not in the sense that I've read all the texts and manuals, attended all the seminars, and know all there is to know about the subject.

All I can really say is that I love stories, I tell stories, and when I do, people lean forward and listen and seem to love those stories too. So what I can share are the tips and techniques and, particularly, the attitudes and approaches I have picked up along the way. I can tell you what has worked and what has failed, where I find stories, and how I tear them apart and put them back together again as I prepare to tell them. And if you're willing to accept, from the start, that all storytellers are different, and that their storytelling is as much a reflection of their personality as it is of the stories themselves, then I think we can go somewhere together. So if you find something that's helpful along the way – brilliant! And if something else just won't work for you – then that's all right too. Because that's how I learned to tell stories. By watching and listening, trying and failing, and starting all over again!

So let's start with how it all began.

Child's Play

When I was twelve, my younger brother, Tim, came home one afternoon, desperate to do something in the School Talent Show. He found a Muppet pattern in a women's magazine (you can tell how long ago that was – *Sesame Street* was brand new, then!), and stitched together a few puppets on my grandmother's old sewing machine. All he needed was a script. So I wrote one for him. I can't honestly remember what it was about, but it began an eight-year run of puppet shows in churches and camps and community festivals in the Pittsburgh area.

My other brother, Daryl, and a few other friends joined in as well. And my mum ferried us around in her beaten-up old Studebaker. We were just kids, but that experience taught us a lot about storytelling.

We discovered, first of all, how important it is to have interesting characters. Tim is a natural comedian, and very quick-witted, so it didn't take us long to start building the stories around the puppets that he controlled. We countered his cheeky irreverence with a collection of "straight man" type characters – typical stand-up fare – which helped us learn the place of conflict in storytelling too. Bit by bit, we discovered the ways that characters can work together to create both humour and tension, and build the story to a satisfying conclusion.

We also learned how important it is to build a relationship with an audience. Puppeteers can only tell how their audiences are reacting through what they hear. We discovered, very quickly, how helpful it is to see those reactions as well. So we started putting someone "out front", at the side of the stage, to be our eyes. He would sometimes act as a narrator, sometimes as a straight man, sometimes even as one of the characters. But, best of all, he would watch the crowd, gauge their reactions, and move things on or slow things down, depending on what he saw.

We learned a lot about story pacing and story length as well. Our early stories were short and punchy, largely because we were pretty insecure and wanted to get in there and get out as quickly as possible! But as our confidence grew, so did the stories. And that was a mistake. It was the era of rock opera, and I suppose I fancied myself in that light – writing huge puppet extravaganzas. But they just didn't work. They meandered on and on, losing their point and their tension, and worst of all, the audience! To this day, I would still rather do several short stories than one long one – because it gives me the chance to adapt and adjust (or simply bail out!) instead of being stuck in the middle of some epic.

Yes, we made mistakes – loads of them! Inadequate practice. Incomprehensible messages (more than one parent or teacher or pastor wanted to know what "that story was about"). And inappropriate humour (although I still wet myself over most things scatalogical!). But the most important thing was that we learned from those mistakes and we improved, year by year.

There's one thing I can't emphasize enough – the only way you learn to tell stories and improve your storytelling abilities is to do it. Because I'm an author, people often ask me, "How do I get a book published?" My usual response is, "What have you written?" And you would be amazed at how many of them haven't written anything at all! Sometimes it's fear, and sometimes it's uncertainty, and sometimes it's a lack of confidence. And I understand all those feelings, because I've been there, myself. But unless you actually put those things behind you and have a go, you'll never write a book. And the same thing is true of storytelling. You have to try, accepting from the start that you'll make mistakes, face difficult audiences, forget where you're going, and not always get it right. But you have to start somewhere. You have to take that leap. Maybe it's because we were just kids, and didn't know any better – but we had a go. And because we had a go, we learned a lot about telling stories.

University Challenge

I learned a lot about stories at university, too. I was studying theology, preparing for a career in the ministry, and was surprised to discover that this helped me to understand even more about the way that stories work and the power they have to affect us.

The Bible is essentially a collection of stories. It contains other genres, I know, but the bulk of the Bible relates events in the history of Israel and then in the life of Jesus – stories that are meant to help us understand both who God is and who we are. Preaching, therefore, has a lot to do with storytelling. Yes, I tried some of the other approaches – three points and a conclusion, unpacking the apostle Paul's tightly knit theological arguments, wrestling with the imagery in the psalms. But what I discovered, even in the churches where I preached as a student, was that people responded best to stories. They leaned forward, they listened, they laughed, they cried – they got the point! So I just kept on telling stories. And not just as illustrations so much as for the Bible stories themselves.

One of my biggest inspirations in this regard was a book I stumbled across in the seminary library while I was doing some research for one of my preaching homiletics classes. The book was called *Telling the Truth*, but what really caught my attention was the subtitle – *The Gospel as Tragedy, Comedy and Fairy Tale*. It was written by American Frederick Buechner, who is both an award-winning novelist and a theologian. Buechner's premise is pretty simple. Preaching is all about telling stories. It starts with recognizing the tragic stories that are a part of each of our lives – by acknowledging them and taking them seriously. It moves on to the comedy of the gospel – the holy foolishness of a God who speaks his light and laughter into that tragedy. And it finishes with what Buechner calls the truest fairy tale of them all. He contrasts the story of the Wizard of Oz with the gospel story. In the former, there is no magic in the end – nothing beyond our own power to redeem ourselves, just a man pulling levers behind a curtain and a lot of self-belief. But in the gospel, Buechner argues, we find true magic – a power at work in us that accomplishes what we could never have done for ourselves.

Buechner's book excited me in a way that no other book on preaching had ever done before (or has done since). It convinced me that I could be a preacher and a storyteller, taking the thing I loved and weaving it into my calling. And that's what I took to my first church.

As it happens, my first church was in Leicestershire, in the UK (how I got there from a seminary in the hills of East Tennessee is a story in itself – or maybe the makings of a country and western song). And, to be fair, telling Bible stories there was a bit of a challenge, at first, because the people in that church were older, on the whole, had mostly been raised in Sunday school and had already heard a lot of those stories. I'm not complaining. I think it's marvellous when Christians know a lot about the Bible. It's how things should be. But, on the other hand, there's nothing worse than that "Oh, here's THAT story, again" look. As any parent knows, you can tell the same story to a small child time and time again. But it's different with older children and adults. A familiar story is a lot like a joke when you've already heard the punchline; you know how it's going to end, so you don't pay as much attention along the way. It's the old "been there, done that" thing.

So I had to work a little harder to find a way around that problem. If I were retelling a familiar Bible story, I tried my best to find a unique way "in" to the story. Sometimes I told it from a different perspective (from the "bad guy's" point of view, perhaps!). Sometimes I introduced a character who could be an objective observer of all that went on. Sometimes I started the story at an unfamiliar place. Anything to keep the listeners guessing, so that when they finally realized which story it was, they were interested enough to see how that particular slant would bring them round to the ending. There's nothing original about this of course – the spate of reworked and re-imagined fairy tales that have appeared over the last several years, both in print and on film, attests to the fact that this works with other kinds of stories as well. And that's the important thing – it re-establishes the kind of tension and expectancy that pulls an audience through a story.

The other thing that preaching in my first church taught me was the way that an audience relates to the characters in a story. Many people who aren't familiar with the Bible assume that it's a pious, holier-than-thou kind of book. The fact of the matter is that the Bible is brutally honest about the people whose lives it chronicles. We see them – even the "heroes" – warts and all. And that means that people can identify with the characters in a Bible story, both at their best times and at their worst. Because the stories are human and honest, they encourage people to be honest about themselves.

One Sunday, I told the story of the prodigal son, and when the service had finished, one of our older ladies said that she wanted to talk with me about the message, some time during the coming week. A few days later I went to visit her, and following the obligatory tea and cakes and snooker match (that's right, for some reason, in the mid-eighties, all my elderly parishioners were glued to the TV in the afternoon, watching snooker. Steve Davis was, of course, their hero – "What a nice young man" – and the villainy usually came in the form of the late Alex Higgins), she proceeded to tell me (as if she were addressing the diabolical Alex himself) how much she had disliked my sermon. I couldn't for the life of me see the problem, and I couldn't get a word in edgeways – and then came the punchline. "When I was a young woman," she explained, "all my brothers and sisters moved away and left me at home to care for my parents. I was like the son who stayed with his father, but when you told the story, you did what everyone does – you turned him into the villain!"

That made everything clear. Stories invite us to relate to particular characters, but a storyteller can't control the choice that someone makes in that respect. So we talked about the story again and how the mercy shown by the father extended to the older son as well – and could also extend to her.

Ministry to Museum

My children were both born in England, and when that ministry came to an end, we moved back to Pittsburgh, primarily so that my wife and I could raise the kids near their extended family. My brother, Tim, was working in children's theatre at the time, but was interested in developing his career in a new direction. He had done some storytelling at one of the big Pittsburgh libraries and thought that, by telling stories together, he and I could recreate the same dynamic that had worked so well with the puppets, years before. So I took a "break" from the ministry and joined him.

We took one of the stories he had been telling – "Joe Magarac", Pittsburgh's tall tale about a heroic steel worker – and adapted it to our own style. What we came up with was a kind of "tag team" approach to storytelling, taking it in turn to tell the narrative. Sometimes we would cross over into drama, with each of us taking different "parts". And sometimes it would look more like a stand-up comedy routine as we borrowed the "straight man", "funny man" stuff from our puppet days.

I suppose the purist would argue that it wasn't straightforward storytelling. And it wasn't. It was a fusion of a lot of different styles and approaches. But the bottom line was that it worked! Kids loved it. Teachers did too. And I continued to learn more about telling stories.

First of all, I learned about the importance of structure, control and rules in a storytelling context. This was essential for our work in school assemblies. In the US, these usually last for 45–50 minutes, and are made up of either the whole school together, or the school broken into two big groups (corresponding roughly to Infants and Juniors in the UK). So the average session was two to three hundred children, although I can recall times when that number jumped to five or six hundred! In addition, we were usually working in rooms that were not the best, acoustically – barn-sized gymnasiums where the sound echoed everywhere or ancient auditoriums with squeaky folding seats. In that kind of a situation, we found that we needed some way to keep the children as quiet as possible, or to re-establish that quiet following some participation activity that we had instigated!

In his children's theatre work, Tim had come across a device that many teachers use – and we found that it worked for us, as well. He started each programme by telling the children that they were going to have a great time. They would see things that they liked, and maybe even things that they didn't like. But most of all, they would see things that made them laugh, and perhaps make them want to say something to their neighbour. He assured them that we understood that, but also pointed out that too much of that kind of noise would make it hard to hear the story. Then Tim would stick his arm straight up in the air. (He's a tall guy – so if the room was low, he would sometimes smack his hand up against the ceiling. The kids loved that!) "When you see the hand go up," Tim would say, "then everyone needs to get quiet as quickly as possible and look straight up here."

And that was it. It seems simple, I know. Almost too simple to work! But it did. And I think it did precisely because it was so simple.

The device was just a way of giving us room to work and the opportunity to be heard in the first place. With rowdier groups, we had to reinforce it more at the start – so that they would get the idea, and understand that we really meant it. And, yes, there was the odd occasion when we did have to give in and simply carry on in spite of the noise. But 97 per cent of the time it worked. And it worked because – just as we'd promised – the kids really were enjoying themselves.

During this time, I also learned a lot about respecting children. Tim and I often had the chance to listen to other storytellers and, sadly, some of them felt the need to adopt that sickly sweet tone of voice when talking to children. Perhaps I'm being too hard here, but it seems to me that children (older children in particular) feel that they are being "talked down to" when they hear that tone. We were determined, from the start, to talk to children in our natural voices – to just be ourselves when we were with them. I think that showed respect and that we valued them. And it was probably one of the reasons that we received their respect in return.

This approach helped to engage teachers in our stories as well. Quite often, teachers would get the kids settled for the beginning of the assembly, and then mark papers or do some other kind of work while the assembly was going on. Tim and I decided that one of our goals would be to get the teachers to put away their work and listen! Tossing in the odd adult reference or joke certainly helped, but so did the fact that we didn't talk down to the kids and made it clear that the stories we told were for "everybody".

Finally, I think I learned a lot about simplicity. Many of the schools we visited had hosted assemblies that required elaborate lighting and sets. And with certain kinds of productions, that's necessary. But it isn't with storytelling. In fact, Tim and I agreed, early on, that we would take no more into an assembly than what the two of us could carry in one trip (or that would squeeze into the back of his Honda)! That meant the obligatory cup of coffee in one hand, and a stool, or a coat rack, or a plastic dustbin full of props in the other. We took it in turn to sit on the stool. We used a few props for each programme. And the coat rack? Well, as we enjoyed explaining to the kids during the question and answer session – that was for hanging our coats on! And it gave a bit of a backdrop – a concession, I suppose to the comments we would sometimes overhear: "You mean we spent hundreds of dollars for this?!" The assumption, of course, was that a presentation without lots of fancy props and sets and lights couldn't possibly engage the children. But that assumption was wrong. Storytelling doesn't require anything but engaged imaginations. Not even coat racks and dustbins. And we proved that, time and time again.

A little girl – not more than seven or eight years old – came up to me after a session, once, and her comments say it all. "That story you told," she said – her eyes full of wonder, "I could see it! I could see everything! The old man, the mountain, the waves. I could see it!" In an age when we bombard our children with visual and aural stimulation, it's a real thrill to hear those words. Because, given half a chance, children's imaginations can run free – like they were meant to. And they can see! They really can. If only we're willing to keep things simple.

Tim and I toured for a year on our own, and then were spotted by the Schools Outreach Director of The Pittsburgh Children's Museum at a performers' showcase. She asked us to become a part of their team, representing them in schools, which we did for the next ten years. We carried on telling "Joe Magarac", but then went on to create five more storytelling programmes (none of them Bible-based, because of the separation of church and state in US government-funded schools). This took us to the magic number of six – "magic" because six is the number of grade levels in the average American elementary school. And that means that you can go back to the same school, year after year, and never have to repeat a programme with the same audience!

Here's a summary of our six programmes:

1. Joe Magarac, the traditional Pittsburgh tall tale.

2. "Construct-a-Tale" illustrated the basics of good story construction (character, setting, and problem) through the telling of a traditional French fairy tale, "How Johnny Pancake Did Not Marry the Princess of France".

3. "Goal tending" was so-named because Pittsburgh is a big ice hockey town. It was based on *The One and Only Delgado Cheese*, a story about

making dreams come true and one of the first books I wrote.

4. "Anderson Choose" was based on an original fairy tale that Tim and I wrote together. It focused on citizenship and making good choices.

5. "Folk Trails" bound together three traditional tales as a way of demonstrating how different cultures share and communicate values through story, and how similar those values often are.

6. "Tales That Tell Why" was all about science. This was a real stretch, as it wasn't exactly our strongest subject in school and we struggled to find a way to deal with science in a storytelling context. We finished up contrasting the scientific method (as illustrated by the lives of Ptolemy, Copernicus, and Galileo) with traditional stories that tried to explain how things came to be.

Looking back on it, it's strange to think that all those stories (and quite a few more, actually) were bouncing around in our heads at one time – particularly since I'm not that great at memorizing. Maybe that will be an encouragement, if that's your situation too. There's no better way to get really comfortable with a story, and plumb the depths of its power and effectiveness, than by telling it again and again and again. And I can say with confidence that we told some of those stories hundreds of times and more!

At the same time, however, we were both involved in individual pursuits. I took up writing books for children, and Tim landed better and better acting jobs, both on stage and in film. (He has now appeared in two Broadway shows and had parts in several films.) In the end, the time came when we needed to give more attention to those other pursuits. So Tim carried on with his acting, and I moved to the UK to promote my books, tell stories in schools, and teach others how to tell stories, too.

The Big Spender

Earlier in this chapter, I described the conversation I had with one of my elderly parishioners regarding the parable of the prodigal son. I thought it would be appropriate, therefore, to include one of the retellings I have done of that story. This one is from *The Lion Storyteller Bible*, but you can find different retellings in *Telling the Bible* and in *Telling the Gospel*. In fact, in *Telling the Bible*, there is a retelling called "The Other Prodigal", which is told from the point of view of the elder son. I guess it was my way of addressing my parishioner's concerns.

Telling tips: *Divide the group into three parts – younger son, father, and older son. Teach the "younger son" group the line "I want my money now!" Teach the "father" group the line "You are my son!" And teach the "older son" group the line "It's not fair!" Then lead them in saying the line with feeling at the appropriate part of the story.*

The people who thought they were good were still not happy with Jesus. They moaned. They grumbled. They frowned.

"It's not fair," they complained. "Jesus spends all his time with the bad people."

Jesus heard this and told them one more story:

"Once upon a time there was a man who had two sons. He loved them both, very much. But one day, the younger son came to him with a sad request.

'Father,' the younger son said, 'when you die, I will get part of your money and part of your land. The problem is, I don't want to wait. I want my money now!'

It was all the father could do to hold back his tears. But because he loved his son, he agreed, and gave him his share of the money.

That very day the son left home, money in his pocket and a big smile on his face. He didn't even say goodbye. The father just watched, wiped away a tear, and hoped that one day he would see his son again.

The son travelled to a country far, far away and spent his money just as fast as he could. He drank. He gambled. He used his money to do many bad things – until finally the money was gone.

The son looked for a job, but the only work he could find was taking care of pigs! It was hard, dirty work, and he was so hungry sometimes that he thought about taking the pigs' food for himself. He was miserable, lonely and sad. And then one day, he had an idea.

'The servants who take care of my father's animals are much happier than me. I'll go home, that's what I'll do. I'll tell my father how sorry I am for wasting his money. And maybe, just maybe, he'll let me become a servant and work for him.'

Now what do you think the father had been doing all this time? Did he say to himself, 'I have my eldest son at home with me. Who cares if my younger son is gone?' Of course not! He loved his son, even though he had gone far away. And every day, he would go out to the roadside and watch, hoping his son would return.

That's exactly where he was when the younger son hobbled home, poor and hungry. The father ran to his son and hugged him tight. And the son dropped right to his knees.

'Oh, Father,' he cried. 'I'm so sorry. I have wasted all your money and am no longer good enough to be your son.'

'Don't be silly,' said his father. 'You are my son. You will always be my son. And I am so glad to have you back!' Then the father lifted his son to his feet and walked him home. He dressed him in beautiful clothes. He put gold rings on his fingers. And he threw him a big welcome home party.

When the elder son came home from work that night, he heard the party noise.

'What's happening?' he asked. And when a servant told him, he was filled with anger and ran to his father.

'It's not fair!' he shouted. 'I've been a good son. I've worked hard for you all these years. But he was bad. He wasted your money. And now you're throwing him a party.'

'I love you, my son,' the father said. 'And you have enjoyed all the good things I have. But your brother was gone and now he's back. He was lost and now he's found. That's why I'm having this party, because we're all back together again.'"

Joe Magarac – The Steel Man

Here's a version of the story that my brother and I chose as the first of our storytelling assemblies. It's a less well-known example of a story genre that is unique to the US – the tall tale. Pecos Bill, Paul Bunyan and John Henry are other examples of this kind of legendary story that emerged in the States during the nineteenth century. These tales usually celebrate specific occupations and regions, and because Pittsburgh was built on steel, and on the labour of men and women who came from all over Europe to work in its mills, this story is about a man of Hungarian origin who was literally made of steel.

Telling tips: *Everyone "plays" Joe Magarac, repeating the actions after you, as appropriate. They stamp on the floor – Boom! Boom! Boom! – make a rumbling tumbling laugh, and hee-haw like donkeys. They also pretend to gobble up coal, drink steel soup, and pick their teeth with chisels. Then they pick up the railroad tracks and stir and squeeze the steel to make beams – with you leading the way and providing the example.*

One by one, the steel-working men huffed and puffed and struggled to lift the long steel beams. It was a contest – a contest that took place once a year in the smoky shadow of the steel mill – to prove who was the strongest man in the steel-making valley.

But as the light of the setting sun mingled with the blast-furnace soot and fire, not a man among them had yet been able to lift the heaviest beam of all.

Suddenly they heard something – Boom! Boom! Boom! Then they felt the earth shake. And finally, they saw him, tramping through the twilight, hammering the ground with his steel-tipped shoes – a giant of a man, nine feet tall at least, with hands like shovels and a head full of burnt brown hair!

He lumbered through the crowd, right up to the heaviest steel beam. Then he wrapped one hairy fist around it – and swung it up over his head!

The crowd gasped. They had never seen anyone so strong. But the big man just tilted back his head and laughed – a rumbling, tumbling sound, like steel makes as it bubbles and boils in the furnace.

"Let me introduce myself," he roared. "My father was the sun, hotter than any furnace. My mother was Mother Earth herself. And I was born in the belly of an ore-bearing mountain. For I am a man who is made of steel! And my name is Joe Magarac."

Now it was the crowd's turn to laugh. For in their language, the word "magarac" meant "donkey"!

"Laugh all you want," the big man chuckled. "Because all I want to do is eat like a donkey and work like a donkey!"

The steel-working men laughed again, and clapped and cheered. Then they gathered round Joe and introduced themselves.

But high in the steel mill, in the fancy room where the bosses worked, there was another man – the Big Boss, the man who owned the steel mill.

His face was pressed to the window and, through the grime and the smoke, he could see what was going on in the yard below.

"He's a strong man," the Big Boss smiled. "So I will hire him to work for me. Then maybe I won't need to hire so many other men."

Joe started every day in the same way. He gobbled up a bucket of coal and washed it down with a bowl of steaming, hot steel soup. Then he tramped over to the mill, picking his teeth with a hard cold chisel.

He grabbed a pile of old railroad tracks with one arm, and ten tons of iron ore with the other. Then he carried them over to Furnace Number Nine and dumped them in. And finally he shovelled coal underneath and set the whole thing burning with a finger-snap spark.

The stuff inside the furnace started to melt. It turned red and orange and yellow and white hot.

But that heat didn't bother Joe. No, he stuck his arm in there and stirred it around. "Kind of tickles," he laughed.

And then, as that stuff cooled down, thick and gooey, Joe grabbed a handful in his fist and squeezed it tight. And out between his fingers oozed four perfect steel beams!

Day by day, week by week, month by month, those beams piled up. Until the warehouses were full. And the steel yard. And, at last, the mill itself.

And that's when the Big Boss came down from his fancy room.

"Boys!" he hollered. "I got some bad news for you. Joe Magarac, here, has made so much steel, we're not gonna need any more for a while. So I want you to go home. I'll call you if I want you to work again."

The steel-working men walked slowly home. No work meant no money. And that meant no food on the table or shoes on their children's feet.

They turned and looked back at the mill. No furnace firelight dancing against the windowpanes. No clouds billowing black out of the smokestacks. Nothing but stillness and sadness and rust.

And inside the mill there was only Joe, sitting in Furnace Number Nine, a little steel tear running down his big steel cheek.

"This is my fault," he whispered to the dirty walls. "I ate like a donkey and worked like a donkey, and now my friends have no jobs. I must do something to help them."

The clocks in the houses of the steel-working men ticked away hours and days and weeks and months. Their families were hungry. Their hopes were fading. And then, one night, just as the clock struck nine, they saw it, down in the valley – a furnace burning in the mill!

They rushed out of their houses and down the crooked hillside streets. They burst into the mill itself. And that's when they heard it – the very same sound they'd heard on the night that Joe came tramping through the twilight – the rumbling, tumbling sound that steel makes as it bubbles and boils in the furnace.

They followed that sound and it led them to Furnace Number Nine. And there, in the furnace, was the head of Joe Magarac, floating on a white-hot pool of steel.

"Joe! Get out of there!" they shouted.

But Joe just laughed. "Don't worry about me," he said. "I was the reason you lost your jobs. And now I'm gonna fix that. When I am all melted down, I want you to pour me out into steel beams, 'cause my steel is the strongest steel there is. Then I want you to tear down this old mill and use my beams to make a new one. A bigger one. One that will make jobs for you and your children for years to come!"

The big man said, "Goodbye!" and then the head of Joe Magarac disappeared into the boiling steel and he was never seen again.

The men did what Joe had told them, and the next year there was another strong man contest in the new steel yard. And the prize? It was the privilege of tending the fires in Furnace Number Nine – the furnace where Joe Magarac had sacrificed himself for everyone in the steel-making valley.

The Big Wave

This is the story that the little girl said she could "see", even though there weren't any actual images. Well, apart from the ones in her head.

This is another story that Tim and I incorporated into one of our assembly shows, and I still use it quite a bit today. In fact, I think it's a really effective way of getting across the nature of sacrifice, so I often tie it into the passion of Jesus.

It helps that the story is a true one. A British writer called Lafcadio Hearn, who lived in Japan in the nineteenth century and collected and translated stories from that culture, brought it to the West originally.

Telling tips: *You might want to ask your audience to play the people in the village. You could divide them into lots of little groups – old men and young men and mothers and grandmothers and babies and boys and girls – and have them say "hello!" in appropriate voices (except for the babies of course, who will go "Waaa!") when they are introduced in the story. They can then make "party" noises (singing, perhaps – a simple tune) while the old man watches them. And finally they can pound their feet on the floor as they run up the hill.*

Alternatively, they could play the wave – pounding their feet on the floor lightly when the old man first sees it, and then more and more loudly when it rushes towards the village and finally hits it with a crash.

The sea splashed gently against the sandy beach. The sandy beach lay white and hot before the little village. And in the little village lived four hundred people – old men and young men, mothers and grandmothers, babies and boys and girls.

Behind the village, green terraces rose like steps to a high, flat plateau. And on the plateau stood a fine old house, surrounded by rice fields.

In that house lived Hamaguchi – an old man, a rich man, owner of the rice fields and lord of the village below. With him lived his grandson – only ten years old, full of questions, and full of life.

One hot summer evening, Hamaguchi walked slowly out onto his porch. He looked at the village below, and smiled. It was harvest time, and his people were celebrating with music and dancing and bright lantern lights.

He looked at the beach beyond, cool and quiet and calm, and he smiled again.

But when Hamaguchi looked out across the sea, his smile turned suddenly to a worried frown. For there was a wave, a wave that stretched as far as he could see, tall and wild and fierce. And it was rushing towards the village below.

Hamaguchi had never seen this kind of wave. But he had heard tales about such waves from his father and his father's father. So he called his grandson and asked him to bring a flaming torch.

"Why, Grandfather?" the boy asked innocently. "Why do you want a torch?"

"There is not time to explain," Hamaguchi answered. "We must act quickly!" And he hobbled to the fields on the left of the house and set his crops on fire.

"Grandfather!" the boy cried. "What are you doing?"

Hamaguchi looked down at the village. No one was looking up at the plateau.

"There is no time!" he barked. "Come with me." And he took the boy by the hand and set fire to the fields on the right.

The flames burst orange and yellow and white against the night, and the boy began to weep.

"Grandfather, are you mad? This is everything you own!"

But the old man said nothing. He looked down at the village, then hurried to the remaining fields and set the torch to them, as well. The sky was filled with sparks and smoke and the little boy was sobbing now.

"Please, Grandfather! Stop, Grandfather! There will be nothing left!"

Just then, a bell sounded, ringing from the temple in the village below. And soon, streaming up the terraced hill, came the villagers – young women, old women, boys and girls, fathers and grandfathers, babies on their backs and buckets in their hands. All four hundred of them – running to help put out the fire!

And, just as they reached the burning fields, the wave struck the village below.

It sounded like thunder.

It sounded like cannon fire.

It sounded like the hoof-beats of ten thousand horses.

It destroyed everything in its path, and when at last it rumbled and rolled back out to sea, there was not a single house left standing.

The people looked in horror at the ruins of their village. But when at last they turned to face the fields, they were gone as well – burned to the ground.

Hamaguchi's grandson grabbed him round the waist and, sobbing still, asked the question everyone else wanted to hear.

"Why, Grandfather? Why did you burn down your precious fields?"

"Don't you see?" the old man said to the crowd. "I had to find some way to warn you – to lead you out of harm's way. For, as precious as my fields are to me, each and every one of you is more precious still."

And with that, Hamaguchi invited them all to stay in his house until the village was rebuilt.

The old man lived many more years, but when at last he died, the people built a little shrine in their village, in memory of the lord who sacrificed all he had to save them from the terrible wave.

The One and Only Delgado Cheese

Here's another tale that formed the basis of one of our storytelling assemblies. It's an original story – in fact, the first book I wrote for Lion Publishing, way back in the early nineties. It's been out of print for ages, so I thought this was a good excuse to bring it back into circulation again.

Telling tips: *This is one to tell on your own.*

Harvey Merritt was not the kind of boy that people noticed.

Harvey was not bright enough for people to say, "Oh, what a clever child!"

Harvey was not good enough at football for people to say, "Oh, what an athletic child!"

Harvey was not especially tall, nor extremely short. He wasn't ugly. He wasn't cute. He was just plain normal. And he didn't like that one bit.

So when he moved from the Warren G. Harding School to the Edward Everett Horton Elementary School, Harvey decided to do something about it.

One Monday morning, when Harvey walked into his new school, he saw a sign hanging on the bulletin board.

"TALENT SHOW," the sign said: "SIGN UP NEXT FRIDAY AFTERNOON."

Now, as you may have guessed, Harvey Merritt was not particularly talented, either. But his desire to be noticed was so great, he was determined to find *something* that he could do.

Harvey's first step was to talk with his Great Uncle Kaz.

Great Uncle Kaz was the reason Harvey's family had moved in the first place. He had to stay in a wheelchair and needed someone to look after him and his big house. Someone who could cook and clean. And someone who didn't mind the occasional bursts of what Uncle Kaz called his "preachy-telling" (and what his relatives called his "funny ways").

Great Uncle Kaz stayed by himself most of the time in his faded, musty bedroom at the back of the house, thumbing through his Bible and preachy-telling his stories to the wallpaper birds – or to Harvey, who often wandered in for a game of checkers and ended up listening to "How the Lions Lost their Lunch" or "The Whale's Sour Snack".

As far as Harvey was concerned, those old Bible stories of Daniel and Jonah had never been so interesting. He liked Great Uncle Kaz. In fact, of all the people Harvey knew, he felt most noticed by Great Uncle Kaz.

Uncle Kaz listened patiently to Harvey, nodding his bald, wrinkled head from time to time as Harvey talked about the school talent show poster.

"A talent show, eh? Well, what can you do, Harvey? Can you sing?"

Harvey shook his head, "No."

"Can you dance?"

"No."

"Do you know any good jokes?"

Harvey didn't.

Great Uncle Kaz thought for a moment. Then he got a look in his eye like a preachy-telling was coming on.

"Harvey," he said, "do you see that old trunk beside the bed? Take the blankets off the top, open it, and bring me the first thing you find inside."

The first thing Harvey found was a paper tube with a rubber band around the middle. Uncle Kaz slid off the rubber band and unrolled the paper. It was a poster.

In the middle of the poster, which was now yellow, but which was probably once white, big letters read:

"FROM THE STAGES OF ZANZIBAR, MADRID AND GAY PAREE – DANCIN' DAN THE VAUDEVILLE MAN!"

"Who's that?" Harvey asked.

Uncle Kaz smiled a sly smile. "That was me – years ago."

Harvey looked puzzled. "But Mom said you were some kind of preacher."

The old man chuckled. "The Good Lord gave me a talent, Harvey – a gift for telling stories, for getting folks to sit up and pay attention. But

before the Lord grabbed hold of me to do that for him, I was Dancin'
Dan the Vaudeville Man."

"What's Vaudeville?" asked Harvey.

"It's a bit like your talent show. A lot of people doing a little bit of
everything. Singing, dancing, juggling. Acrobatics, comedy, magic
acts. We weren't the best, but we enjoyed ourselves. That was the most
important thing – for me anyway."

Uncle Kaz stopped. Like a light bulb had switched on in his head.

"Harvey," he said, "the Good Lord gave us all talents. Not all of us the
same ones. Not all of us the same number. But he didn't pass anybody
by. And the road to finding those talents starts with what brings us joy.
Harvey, what do you enjoy?"

Harvey's light bulb lit up, as well. Yes, there was something he
enjoyed doing. He liked to do...

"CARTWHEELS!"

Harvey shouted it, and Uncle Kaz jerked back his head in surprise.

"Cartwheels?" he said.

"Last year, in second grade, we had to learn to do cartwheels. I
couldn't, at first, but I kept trying and trying. And one day, I could. I like
to do cartwheels."

"Then cartwheels it is!" announced Uncle Kaz. "Or at least that will
be the main part of your act."

"The main part?" asked Harvey, a little concerned.

"Sure. You can't just do cartwheels. You've got to build an act around
that. A little juggling. A little magic, maybe. But don't worry, I can teach
you how to do those things. OK?"

Harvey nodded his head, hesitantly, He wasn't sure about those other
things, but he figured he could try. He'd managed cartwheels, hadn't
he? He smiled at Uncle Kaz and headed for the door.

"One more thing," Uncle Kaz called, waving the poster. "You need to
come up with a name. A stage name. Something people will notice."

It was two days before a special name, a really *noticeable* name,
came to Harvey. Mrs Finchley, his teacher, was talking about geography.
And, as usual, Harvey wasn't paying much attention. But somewhere
between the cattle ranches on the Mexican border and the dairy farms

in Wisconsin, he got an idea.

Harvey rushed home and started to draw furiously. Within an hour he had made a poster. He rolled it up, wrapped a rubber band around it, and knocked on his uncle's door.

"What have you go there, behind your back?" asked Uncle Kaz.

"It's a poster," said Harvey. "A poster that people will notice. With a name they'll notice, too." And he slowly unrolled it and held it up.

Uncle Kaz cocked his head to one side and squinted really hard. Then he smiled. And, slowly and proudly he read:

"FROM THE STAGES OF ZANZIBAR, MADRID AND GAY PAREE – THE ONE AND ONLY DELGADO CHEESE!"

"Delgado Cheese," Uncle Kaz repeated. "It's just the name I would have chosen."

"Really?" said Harvey.

"Absolutely! It's… uhhmm… exotic. That's what it is!"

"Exotic?" asked Harvey, a little worried.

"Yes. Strange but wonderful. Like the cherubim and seraphim. Like manna in the wilderness. Like your Aunt Minnie's spoon collection. And now, Mr Delgado Cheese, what say we teach you a few magic tricks?"

Over the next few weeks, Harvey – or Delgado Cheese, as he now preferred to be called – stopped by his Uncle Kaz's room every day after school. It seemed to Harvey that, for some reason, his Uncle Kaz didn't need as much rest as he used to.

With a few items hidden away at the bottom of his trunk, Uncle Kaz showed Delgado Cheese a couple of magic tricks. He also taught him how to juggle three small oranges.

Then they worked hard to combine the magic and the juggling with the cartwheels, so that Delgado had an "act". Delgado's mother joined in too, and made him a silky red shirt with flowing sleeves and pair of bright yellow trousers.

In spite of all that preparation, on the day of the talent show, it was plain to everyone in the house that Delgado Cheese was nervous. So Uncle Kaz asked him into his room. He had a piece of notepaper and a small envelope lying on his lap desk.

"Who will be introducing the performers tonight?" he asked.

"My teacher, Mrs Finchley. Why?"

Uncle Kaz wrote something at the top of the notepaper, folded it, and slid it into the envelope.

"Give this to your teacher, before the show starts," he said.

"OK," said Delgado Cheese. "What is it?"

"It's the *coup de grâce*," grinned Uncle Kaz at a thoroughly puzzled boy. "The rainbow after the flood. The walls of Jericho tumbling down. Lazarus rising up out of his grave. The final touch to what will be your perfect performance."

Delgado stared at his shoes.

"I don't think it's going to be very perfect. I'm really scared."

Uncle Kaz reached over and put one large wrinkled hand on the boy's head. It looked like Delgado was wearing a five-fingered cap.

"Your performance will be wonderful. It will have to be. You're doing what you enjoy. You're using the talents God gave you, right?

"And besides, your mother paid a buck and a half to see the show, and she deserves to get her money's worth."

Delgado looked up. "But what about you? You're coming tonight, aren't you?"

It was Uncle Kaz's turn to look at the floor.

"I haven't had any reason to go out of this house for years," he sighed. "And now that I do, I'm not sure I'm up to it. Maybe I'm like you, Delgado. Maybe I'm just a little scared."

Then he tapped on the note. "You just remember to give this to Mrs Finchley, like I said."

As he waited backstage, Delgado Cheese folded and unfolded the small envelope Great Uncle Kaz had given him. He wanted to give it to Mrs Finchley, but she was busy giving last-minute directions and calming last-minute nerves.

Finally, gulping down his fear and nervousness, Delgado pushed his way past the other performers and thrust the note into his teacher's hands.

"My uncle asked me to give this to you," he said, as loudly as he dared. "He says it's the *coup de grâce*."

Mrs Finchley opened the envelope and quickly read the note to herself.

She smiled.

"Thank you, Harvey. Excuse me... Thank you, Delgado Cheese," she said.

And Delgado Cheese smiled back.

As act followed act, Delgado's fear returned. What did he think he was doing here? What if he goofed? What if he embarrassed himself? He was almost ready to drop his trick cane and his sack of oranges and sneak out, when Mrs Finchley said, "Delgado Cheese, you're on next."

It was too late to run. Too late to go back to being plain old Harvey Merritt.

Mrs Finchley put her hand on his shoulder. "Just one minute," she whispered.

Then she pulled the note from her pocket, stepped up to the microphone and in her best ringmaster's voice announced:

"FRESH FROM THE STAGES OF ZANZIBAR, MADRID AND GAY PAREE, EDWARD EVERETT HORTON ELEMENTARY SCHOOL IS PROUD TO PRESENT THAT JUGGLER, ACROBAT AND MAGICIAN EXTRAORDINAIRE – THE ONE, THE ONLY, DELGADO CHEESE!"

The audience applauded. Mrs Finchley grinned. And Delgado Cheese looked out at the crowd. The lights were so bright that all he could see clearly were the first few rows. But that was all he needed to see. For sitting in his wheelchair, with his top hat and cane, was Dancin' Dan the Vaudeville Man!

Delgado cartwheeled onto the stage. Once for Zanzibar. Twice for Madrid. Three times for Gay Paree. The audience applauded again.

He picked up his oranges and tossed them into the air. One for Zanzibar. Two for Madrid. Three for Gay Paree.

He dropped Zanzibar halfway through, but the people clapped anyway.

Finally, Delgado Cheese reached into his sack and pulled out a magic cane. *Voilà*! Three flowers burst from the end – One for Zanzibar. Two for Madrid. Three for Gay Paree. Then he called Mrs Finchley to his side, reached behind her ear and – *Voilà* again! – pulled out a fifty-cent piece. The audience roared.

Delgado Cheese bowed and smiled. He was using the talents God had given him. He was enjoying himself. At last he was more than just plain normal. He was noticed.

But as he stood there amid the applause, the thing that he noticed most was a wrinkled pair of clapping hands, an old top hat, and a cane – from Zanzibar, Madrid and Gay Paree.

Chapter Two
How Stories "work"

Mr McKee, my sixth-grade teacher, was different from any teacher I'd ever had before. For a start, he was a man, unlike most primary school teachers at that time. And then there was that other thing – the thing that happened, one Friday afternoon, early in the autumn term.

Mr McKee asked us to put away our books and pencils and papers (and let's face it, when you're eleven years old, that request, alone, is enough to make you sit up and take notice!). Then he walked slowly round the room, pulling down the blinds, one by one. Finally, he turned off a few lights so that the room was dark and cool. Everyone looked around. We couldn't imagine what would happen next! And that's when Mr McKee went to the front of the room, reached behind his desk, pulled out a copy of *The Lion, the Witch and the Wardrobe*, and began to read.

As far as I can remember, that's how every Friday afternoon went, for the rest of that term. And we listened, rapt – many of us for the first time – to the adventures of Lucy and Edmund and Peter and Susan, as they wandered through the wardrobe and into the land of Narnia. It was my first exposure to those books. And along with many of my classmates, I rushed to the library afterwards to pick up a copy for myself. But more than that, it was the first time that I ever felt what I now believe lies at the heart of every good storytelling experience. Intimacy. Community. Relationship.

Building Relationships... with the Teller

Before the story itself, before any "tips" and "techniques", good storytelling is all about relationships. And the first and most important relationship is the one that develops between the storyteller and the audience.

To be honest, I have struggled with the term "audience" for some time now, because it suggests a passive group of listeners who simply receive what is offered to them. But there is nothing passive about what happens in a good storytelling session. At the best of times, it is an occasion where the teller and the crowd build something together.

You see, storytelling is not about someone tossing out a mouthful of words for others to catch. It is about that thing that is created between them – the result of imagination and participation and eye contact and laughter and tears. Storytelling is not a presentation, it's a conversation. It's not a performance, it's a dialogue.

Therefore, the same story can be different every time you tell it – because the crowd is different, or the context is different, or the responses are different. During the course of a party, for example, you might say the same things to a number of different people. But the way you say them, the order, the emphasis, will have a lot to do with the way those people respond to you. The same thing is true of storytelling. The crowd thinks that it is watching you, listening to you. But the secret is that you are watching them, listening to them, and responding to them as well!

When my brother and I started telling stories in school assemblies, someone would inevitably try to turn the "house" lights off. I think the assumption was that the children would be quieter in the dark, as they would be in a theatre or a cinema. Well, first of all, if you've ever been in a dark cinema full of kids, you know that's not necessarily the case! But the worst thing was that Tim and I couldn't see them. And seeing them – their responses, their reactions – was essential to building a relationship with them. I have the same problem when it comes to telling stories to very large groups of people – several thousand or so. I'm not saying it can't be done. It's just harder, because the feedback is limited primarily to what I can hear. And when I can see as well, there's just that much more information.

And the more information, the better, because it's all about building that relationship – seeing the crowd's reactions, hearing their responses, shaping the story to suit that particular group. Because if the relationship works, then the story will too.

So how do you build a relationship with a group of people? I think you do it in the same way you would with an individual.

- **Be yourself.** As I said in Chapter 1, resist the temptation to use that "sickly sweet" voice with children or the "pious" voice when you're telling Bible stories. Just be honest about who you are. If you're big and loud and noisy, then your storytelling will probably reflect that. But if you're quieter, then don't try to be something you're not – let your stories reflect that, too.

- **Be confident.** Even if you're shaking inside! Kids, in particular, can smell the fear and the uncertainty. But even with adult groups, everyone feels more comfortable when the person "up front" seems comfortable, too.

- **Be friendly.** Smile as you introduce yourself, or set down the ground rules for the kids. Let them know, right from the start, that this is going to be a good experience, and that everyone is going to have fun.

- **Be smart.** Choose your first story carefully. If I'm doing a half-hour or forty-five minute session, I seldom just do one long story. I do lots of little ones, because that gives me the chance to learn something about the group. I usually start with a story that I know really well, partly because of the "confidence" thing, but more importantly because it gives me the freedom to watch and listen to the crowd. If I'm not thinking about how the story goes or what comes next, I'm free to gauge their responses. Is there a particular kind of humour that they like? Are there a few who are really getting into it? I'll keep my eye on them, and look for a little support, in case things get shaky later! And as for the ones who look as if they want to leave – I remind myself to try something different with them in the next story, because it takes longer for some people to warm to you than others (it's that relationship thing again!). And what if some people never warm to you? Well, stop looking at them and focus instead on the ones who are really enjoying your stuff!

- **Be fun!** Start with something funny – or at least something fun. It's been my experience that most people would rather laugh than cry. So save the serious stuff for later – for just the right moment. It will go down so much better when it comes as a surprise.

"Hang on a minute!" I hear you say. "It's all right for you. You go to lots of different venues and do the same stories each time. What about me? I have to do a different Bible story each week for my school assembly, or Sunday school class, or Bible club. What do I do?"

Well, you have a different set of advantages. You do have to prepare a new story each week, that's true. And in that case, it is more difficult to get really comfortable with the story, as you would with one that you had told a dozen times. But you do have the advantage of knowing your group a lot better than an occasional visitor like me ever will. You know the kind of stories they like, the kind of participation activities they most enjoy. You know who will be up for a bit of "acting along" with you (and who might get totally carried away!). It's the relationship thing again – so use that longer-term relationship – the fact that you really know your group – to your advantage.

I still think it's best to focus on stories that are fun or exciting. That will earn you the right and respect to do that quieter, more serious tale from time to time. And be honest, in that case; there's nothing wrong with saying something like, "Usually we have a bit of a laugh at story time, but this week, we're going to do a really sad or serious story." And then maybe just give them a question to be considering as they listen to you tell it.

Building Relationships... with the Characters

There is another relationship that is important to storytelling. This is the one that develops between those who hear the story and the characters in the story itself. Think of your favourite story. Which character do you like the best? With whom do you identify? One of my clearest childhood memories has to do with a picture book we had of *The Three Little Pigs*. I can remember getting very upset every time the Big Bad Wolf fell down the chimney and landed in the boiling stew pot. I'm not sure what it says about me, but I liked the Big Bad Wolf! (Hey, he worked hard, he stuck to it, he was just doing what wolves do! And that brick-house pig always looked so smug!)

It's this "identification with characters" that makes any good narrative work. Think of your favourite film, your favourite soap opera, your favourite drama or situation comedy. The best ones are always character-driven, because it's the relationship that develops between you and those characters that keeps you watching. And it's true for storytelling, as well. It's like that moment at the end of a good book when you turn over the last page and wish that you could spend just a little more time with those characters. If you have told the story well, then your audience will have identified with one character or another. And better than that, some of them will have accompanied that character on his or her journey and maybe even experienced some sense of discovery or transformation along with that character. And that can be a very powerful experience, indeed.

In his book, *Peace Child*, Don Richardson describes his efforts to tell the story of Jesus to the Sawi tribe in Papua New Guinea. The tribe was known for its cannibalism and its treachery, so when the people in the tribe heard the gospel narrative, the character they most related to was Judas! As you can imagine, this was a real problem for the missionary, who wanted them to understand what Jesus had done and that Jesus was the real hero of the story. Fortunately, the Sawi also had a tradition which they used to deal with the treachery. One tribe would offer another tribe one of its own children to be raised by that tribe, and that exchange would bring the treachery to an end. That child was called the peace child – and when Richardson explained that Jesus was God's peace child to make things right between him and his world, the Sawi understood. All because they were now able to relate to that character!

I am convinced that storytelling has the power to shape and change lives. It really can lead to new discoveries – new ways of thinking and acting. And that brings us to the third significant relationship in storytelling – the relationship of storytelling to a particular community.

Building Relationships... with One Another

Traditionally, storytelling was the means by which values, histories and cultural expectations were passed from one generation to another. Whether the storyteller was a priest or a bard, the point of the story was not simply to entertain, but also to shape and to teach – to define what was good and bad, what was cowardly and heroic, what was acceptable and unacceptable. Jesus used his parables, for example, to challenge deeply held cultural values and assumptions among the religious establishment of his time.

I always have a little chuckle when I hear film makers argue that cinema has no direct effect on the way that people behave. Either they have no understanding of what they are doing, or they hope that we don't. Film and television are two of the chief means that our modern culture uses to access stories. And stories shape cultures. The proof lies in the enormous amount of money that corporations are willing to invest in all those little stories we call advertisements. Do you think for a minute that they would go on spending that kind of money if they weren't confident that those little stories had the power to change what we buy? Storytelling is powerful precisely because it is subtle and subversive, because it can sneak up on you and surprise you. And that's why it needs to be used responsibly – as a means of building community and not destroying it.

Several years ago, my brother and I told a story about self-sacrifice to a class of eleven-year-olds in a Pittsburgh city school. It was a story we had told successfully on a number of occasions, about a rabbit who gives up his life for a field mouse. When the story was finished, the kids just stared at us for a minute, looks of shock and disbelief on their faces.

"That was stupid!" one of them said, at last. "Why would that bunny die for a field mouse?"

"Yeah," echoed several others in the class. "It doesn't make any sense!"

We tried our best to explain that giving up something you wanted for the good of someone else could be worthwhile. Tim even slipped in a little Bible quote (without referencing it, of course!). "Haven't you ever heard the saying – the best thing someone can do is to give up his life for a friend?" They hadn't.

The fact is, they just didn't "get it". Maybe it was the way we told the story. Maybe it was just that particular group of kids. But we came away from that experience determined to make sure that more of our audiences heard more of those kinds of stories – so that there would be some balance to the "take-what-you-can-get-and-kill-as-many-people-as-you-can-along-the-way" kinds of stories that seem to find their way into too many children's lives.

We quickly discovered that schools were really hungry for that kind of story, because it provides a way of talking about all those "citizenship" and "values" issues that teachers sometimes struggle to communicate, particularly in a way that doesn't sound like they're "preaching". So if you think there's too much violence, intolerance and hatred in your community, there's something you can do about it. You can tell stories – stories that are just as powerful, just as exciting, and just as much fun as all those violent tales – but stories that are about gentleness, forgiveness, peace and love.

And that most definitely includes stories from the Bible!

At every Children's Ministry event I have ever attended, someone has quoted Psalm 78, and with good reason. The early part of this psalm says exactly what I have been saying here – people are shaped by the stories they hear. So we have a responsibility to pass on the best stories, particularly those that deal with the relationship between God and his people. Have a look:

> *O my people, hear my teaching;*
> *listen to the words of my mouth.*
> *I will open my mouth in parables,*
> *I will utter hidden things, things from of old –*
> *what we have heard and known,*
> *what our fathers have told us.*
> *We will not hide them from their children;*
> *we will tell the next generation*
> *the praiseworthy deeds of the Lord,*
> *his power, and the wonders he has done.*
> *He decreed statutes for Jacob*
> *and established the law in Israel,*

which he commanded our forefathers
to teach their children,
so the next generation would know them,
even the children yet to be born,
and they in turn would tell their children.
Then they would put their trust in God
and would not forget his deeds
but would keep his commands.
They would not be like their forefathers –
a stubborn and rebellious generation,
whose hearts were not loyal to God,
whose spirits were not faithful to him.

Psalm 78: 1–8

Do you see it? Not only does the psalmist tell us to pass God's story on to the next generation, he tells us why we should do it. So they will keep his commands – and not mess up like some have done! This is all about shaping a generation, shaping a culture. And there's no point arguing that we have no right to do that. Someone will do that, inevitably – either intentionally or as a by-product. For as long as there are stories, stories will shape cultures. So why not tell the best ones? The ones God himself has given us.

And with that, I feel obliged to take at least some space to mention a group of people who have been doing a splendid job of that in the UK over the last decade. There is lots of excellent work being done in this regard, across the country – many groups committed to passing God's story on to the next generation and making sure that it continues to be, at the very least, a part of our collective cultural consciousness. My favourite group among these is Open the Book. All right, I confess, I'm biased. They use my *Lion Storyteller Bible* as the core source of the stories they tell in schools. And they did ask me to be a patron. But, honestly, I'd be excited about their work if neither of these things had happened – because of the history of their ministry and the way they have gone about putting that Psalm 78 mandate into effect.

Originally, Open the Book was never meant to be a national initiative. A small group of Christians in Bedford felt led to tell the story of the Bible, in order, from Genesis to Acts, to the children in their local schools, over the course of one year. They trained small groups of storytellers, two to three per group, comprised mostly of parents, schools workers, vicars, and pensioners – folks who were available during the day. They learned the stories. They made costumes. They built props (sometimes quite elaborate ones!). And in the first year, they told their stories to children in ten local schools. They didn't preach or even do much unpacking. They just told the stories, and the schools were so pleased with what they did that, the following year, fifteen more schools wanted Open the Book groups. So they recruited more volunteers and trained more storytellers, and word started to get around. I think I can probably take some responsibility for that. Whenever I visited a conference or did a storyteller training, I mentioned what these folks were doing and passed on details for contacting them. And, amazingly, people got in touch. It was such a simple idea – and such a good one – particularly that bit about doing the stories in order. I'm convinced that, even in churches, many Christians don't know the "Big Story" – the overall narrative sweep of the Bible. So they don't know how the individual stories fit in, how they connect to one another, and how they relate. The genius of Open the Book is that the children in their audiences get the story in order, so it's less like *Aesop's Fables* ("Oh, here's a lovely story, children with a lovely message") and more like one big adventure. Which, of course, it is!

The other beautiful thing about the programme is that it has re-energized many people who thought their time for ministry had passed. I think the oldest Open the Book member I have come across was in her nineties (if there's anyone older out there, please do let me know). The wonderful thing (the divinely inspired thing, I think) is that those folks come from a generation where the story was passed on, through vibrant Sunday school programmes – so they know the stories, are passionate about the stories, and are keen for this chance to make a difference in a generation several steps down the line.

Christians across the country began to recognize all of this, and started Open the Book groups in their communities, as well. For the greater part of that time, there was no national organization, no website, no budget (apart from what people raised and gave in their own cities and towns and villages). But the thing kept growing. And at the time of writing this book, there are something like 3,000 storytellers in the programme, telling Bible stories to over 70,000 children each week! There is no question in my mind that this "flood" of Bible stories is making a difference in those schools and communities. The fact that schools, themselves, are now approaching Open the Book groups and asking them to come to them shows that they recognize the value. And in the best cases (and there are plenty of examples) this simple passing on of Bible stories has brought schools and churches and communities together. Telling stories makes a difference!

Stories not only have the power to shape communities, they are also a means by which we can build a sense of community. A lot of communication, these days, requires only a face in front of a screen. But storytelling is all about a face in front of a face – faces together, in fact, sharing laughter and tears, surprise and joy. And today that's not a common experience for many children – or adults, for that matter. True, it's more threatening in some ways than sitting alone in front of your television. You might laugh out loud at the wrong time, or have to wipe a tear from an eye. But it's ultimately more rewarding, for it's a chance to discover (or perhaps rediscover!) what happens when people experience a story together.

I have had many experiences over the years that have brought this to light. I was in a school several years ago, telling a story about a bunch of animals that each had different talents. At the end of the story, I asked the children what their talents were. And in the midst of those answers, one boy simply blurted out, "I'm no good at anything!"

I wasn't sure what to do. I didn't know that boy, but there was someone there who did – a teacher, on the other side of the room. She said, "Liam, I've just marked the maths test, and you did better than anyone in the class!" And, boy, did Liam's expression change, because right there, in that little community that had been brought together by a story, he had the chance to admit something really painful and also to find an answer to that pain.

It's almost like the story is a kind of boat. We climb in together – and yeah, the storyteller steers or mans the sails or whatever needs to happen to get the journey started. But in the best situations, everyone gets to contribute to the journey, each in his or her own way – and we go somewhere together.

It can happen in churches, and in classrooms too, when teachers can find some room in the straightjacket of the National Curriculum (don't get me started!) to sit down and relax with their class around a book. It's also happening in other storytelling groups that are springing up all around the country. And, I'm told, there are still places where storytelling happens in pubs on a regular basis. But why not in hospitals and old people's homes and corporate headquarters, as well? Why shouldn't storytelling have a place wherever people come together? For as we let the stories we hear touch our own stories, we become a part of *each other's* stories. We understand; we sympathize. And hopefully, we experience a deeper sense of community.

Building Relationships... with God

When it comes to biblical storytelling, there is one more relationship to take into consideration. And that's the relationship with God, himself. For God reveals himself through story.

If you were to ask an Ancient Israelite to tell you about God, it is unlikely that he would share some abstract philosophy with you. He might recite a psalm. He might show you a few rules. He might quote you a proverb. But it's most likely that he would tell you a story: "My father Abraham was a wandering Aramean. God called him and promised him that if he would follow him, God would give him a land of his own and descendants to outnumber the stars in the sky or the sands in the sea."

Or she might say: "My people were slaves in Egypt. But God set them free and led them to a land flowing with milk and honey!"

The God of Israel is revealed in the story of Israel. We discover who he is by watching how he deals with his people. God's creative power, his passion for justice, and his patient, steadfast love are all revealed in that story.

And when he chose to reveal himself fully, what did God do? Did he drop an essay down from heaven? Did he pass out a theological tract? No, he came in the person of one man – Jesus – who was not just a good storyteller, but who was, himself, The Story. So that by watching what he did, and listening to what he said, we could understand what God was like. Between "once upon a time" and "happily ever after", between "the beginning" and "the end" – that's where we find the Alpha and the Omega – for God is revealed in story.

That means that biblical storytelling is quite sacred stuff. And quite powerful, too! It's not just a matter of standing in front of a group of kids and hoping to survive the following fifteen minutes. No, that Sunday school room, that school hall, that slot in the middle of the family service – that is sacred ground! For it is an opportunity for God to do what he has done from the start of his relationship with his people – to reveal himself, to show who he is and what he can do – through the story that you tell!

The Wedding at Cana

There are any number of stories I could have chosen to demonstrate the importance of a teller and his crowd "working together" to create the story. In fact, any story that involves participation would do. But this particular form of repetitive story is absolutely dependent upon the audience taking part. It's built for that. I describe the theory behind this form later in the book, when I discuss repetition in general, so there is no need to go into that here. But you do need to know how to tell it.

Telling tips: *Each section is a bit like a verse (only this isn't poetry) made of two repeated sentences. The first three lines in each "verse" are yours to say. I always try to say the line a little differently each time, to keep it interesting and also to milk the line of all its meaning.*

The second three lines are for your group. They also have an action to perform (described in parenthesis at the end of the "verse"). Lead your group in that action each of the three times they say that second line. I find that the repetition gives the crowd the chance to "catch up" if they haven't got it the first time. You will need to start the story by teaching all the actions. It's fun, and it also piques their curiosity – what will this story be about?

Jesus and his mum went to a wedding in Cana;
Jesus and his mum went to a wedding in Cana;
Jesus and his mum went to a wedding in Cana;
The bride and the groom looked just divine.
The bride and the groom looked just divine.
The bride and the groom looked just divine.
(Action – fingers like halo above head)

But halfway through the party, everything went wrong.
But halfway through the party, everything went wrong.
But halfway through the party, everything went wrong.
"Jesus," said his mum. "There's no more wine!"
"Jesus," said his mum. "There's no more wine!"
"Jesus," said his mum. "There's no more wine!"
(Action – pretend to hold wine glass)

"What am I supposed to do, Mum?" said Jesus with a sigh.
"What am I supposed to do, Mum?" said Jesus with a sigh.
"What am I supposed to do, Mum?" said Jesus with a sigh.
"You want a miracle, I know, but it's not yet time."
"You want a miracle, I know, but it's not yet time."
"You want a miracle, I know, but it's not yet time."
(Action – point to wrist, to watch, or to a clock in the room)

But Mary was persistent and she told some passing servants,
But Mary was persistent and she told some passing servants,
But Mary was persistent and she told some passing servants,
"I want to you obey this son of mine."
"I want to you obey this son of mine."
"I want to you obey this son of mine."
(Action – point to self)

"Do you see those six stone jars?" said Jesus to the men.
"Do you see those six stone jars?" said Jesus to the men.
"Do you see those six stone jars?" said Jesus to the men.

"Fill them with water to the top-most line."
"Fill them with water to the top-most line."
"Fill them with water to the top-most line."
(Action – draw pretend horizontal line in air)

So they filled them to the brim, thirty gallons each.
So they filled them to the brim, thirty gallons each.
So they filled them to the brim, thirty gallons each.
In one accord with Jesus' Grand Design.
In one accord with Jesus' Grand Design.
In one accord with Jesus' Grand Design.
(Action – pretend to look at blueprint – arms outstretched, examining motion)

"Now draw some out," said Jesus, "and give it to your master.
"Now draw some out," said Jesus, "and give it to your master.
"Now draw some out," said Jesus, "and give it to your master.
"I think you'll be surprised by what he finds."
"I think you'll be surprised by what he finds."
"I think you'll be surprised by what he finds."
(Action – hand over eyes, looking for something)

So they drew a little out and gave it to their master,
So they drew a little out and gave it to their master,
So they drew a little out and gave it to their master,
And a shiver ran right up and down his spine.
And a shiver ran right up and down his spine.
And a shiver ran right up and down his spine.
(Action – draw spine-shaped line, or just shiver)

"This is isn't water!" he exclaimed. "Nor any cheap old plonk.
"This is isn't water!" he exclaimed. "Nor any cheap old plonk.
"This is isn't water!" he exclaimed. "Nor any cheap old plonk.
"It's the finest Chardonnay. This stuff's sublime!"

"It's the finest Chardonnay. This stuff's sublime!"
"It's the finest Chardonnay. This stuff's sublime!"
(Action – make that fingers from mouth movement)

"Others serve their best wine first," he whispered to the groom.
"Others serve their best wine first," he whispered to the groom.
"Others serve their best wine first," he whispered to the groom.
"But you saved the best for last – you're so refined."
"But you saved the best for last – you're so refined."
"But you saved the best for last – you're so refined."
(Action – pretend to straighten pretend moustache – or twist curly bit at the end – nose in air, of course)

So Jesus did a miracle, the first in a long line –
So Jesus did a miracle, the first in a long line –
So Jesus did a miracle, the first in a long line –
A sign to show he really was divine.
A sign to show he really was divine.
A sign to show he really was divine.
(Action – repeat divine/halo action from first verse)

Pharaoh

Here's part of the big story that an Ancient Hebrew (assuming you could find one) would tell if you asked him about his God. It's taken from *Bible Baddies*. And it's another of my Grandma's favourites. So there, this story has a lot going for it – and an interesting retelling to boot.

Telling tips: *You need to get into the heads of the characters in this one – the magicians and Pharaoh himself – to bring them to life.*

At first it was almost amusing.
   "Did you see those two old men?" Pharaoh chuckled to his magicians.
"They looked like a couple of goats, dragged out of the desert."

"Desert goats!" agreed the first magician.

"Moses and A-a-a-ron," baa-ed the second.

Pharaoh laughed out loud. "And did you hear what they wanted?"

"LET MY PEOPLE GO!" mocked the first magician in a deep and booming voice.

"OR YOU'LL BE IN BIG TROUBLE!" boomed the second.

"THE GOD OF THE HEBREWS DEMANDS IT!" boomed Pharaoh too. And they all laughed together.

Pharaoh wiped his eyes. "I suppose I should cut off their heads," he chuckled. "But everyone needs a good laugh, now and then. And I've got to admit it, two desert tramps demanding that I, the supreme ruler of all Egypt, release some stupid Hebrew slaves is the funniest thing I've heard in a long time!"

"Ridiculous!" agreed the first magician.

"The craziest thing I ever heard!" added the second.

No one was laughing the next day, however, when Moses and Aaron walked up to Pharaoh as he strolled along the River Nile.

"Not you again!" Pharaoh sighed.

And his two magicians sighed with him.

"The Lord God has sent us," Aaron explained. "You refused to let his people go and so now, by his power, I will turn the waters of Egypt to blood!"

The magicians couldn't help it. They grinned, they chuckled, they burst into laughter. But when Aaron touched his staff to the river, the smiles dropped from their faces, for the water was blood red.

"How did he do that?" Pharaoh whispered to his magicians.

"It's a… a… trick," stuttered the first magician.

"A-anyone can do it," explained the second.

"Then show me," Pharaoh growled.

The magicians hurried off and managed to find a bowl of clear water. Then they walked slowly back to their master, careful not to spill a single drop. They said their secret words. They shook their sacred sticks. And the water in the bowl turned to blood, as well.

"See," said a more confident Pharaoh to Moses and Aaron. "Anyone can do it!"

"Anyone," agreed the first magician, with a relieved sigh.

"Anyone at all!" boasted the second.

"And so," Pharaoh concluded. "You can tell your god that I will not let his people go."

Seven days later, however, Moses and Aaron came to visit Pharaoh once again.

"This is starting to annoy me," he muttered.

"And me, as well," agreed the first magician.

"Peeved, that's what I am," added magician number two.

But all Aaron said was "Frogs."

"Frogs?" repeated a puzzled Pharaoh.

"Frogs?" echoed his two magicians.

"Frogs," said Aaron once again. "Because you would not let his people go, our God will send frogs. Frogs in your houses. Frogs in your streets. Frogs all over your land." And with that, Aaron waved his staff over the Nile and walked away.

Pharaoh glanced around. "I don't see any frogs," he grunted.

"No frogs here," shrugged the first magician.

But the second magician simply said, "Ribbit."

"That's not funny," Pharaoh growled.

"It wasn't me – honest," the second magician pleaded. Then he lifted up his robe and pointed to his feet. "It was him!"

The frog hopped slowly away. And then, all at once, an army of frogs poured out of the Nile to join him.

Pharaoh and his magicians ran as fast as they could – away from the river, away from the frogs. But when they hurried into the palace, the frogs were there as well. Frogs on the floor, frogs on the furniture, frogs in the cups and plates and bowls!

"A simple trick," panted the first magician.

"We can make frogs too," added the second.

"I'm so pleased to hear it," Pharaoh grumbled. "But can you make them go away?"

The magicians looked at one another, and then sadly shook their heads.

"Then fetch me Moses and Aaron," Pharaoh sighed. "I think it's time to give them what they want."

So Pharaoh told Moses and Aaron that he would set the Hebrews – God's chosen people – free. Aaron smiled and raised his staff and the frogs all died.

But once they were gone, Pharaoh went back on his word, and refused to let the Hebrews go.

So that is why the plagues continued, each one worse than the one before. And that is also why the magicians came to Pharaoh, at last, with a message they knew he would not want to hear.

"Your Majesty," the first magician began, "these plagues can only be the work of some very powerful god. You must stop the suffering. You must let the Hebrews go."

"First there were the gnats," moaned the second magician. "In our eyes and in our ears and up our noses!"

"And then there were the flies," added the first magician. "In our food and in our clothes and in our beds."

"And then the animals died," sniffled the second magician. "The camels and the horses and the cows."

"And now these boils!" groaned the first magician.

"Stop your whingeing!" shouted Pharaoh, as he struggled to his feet. "Do you think that I am blind? That my family and I have not suffered as well? We, too, have swatted gnats and flies. We, too, have watched our animals die. And we, too, are now covered with these crippling sores. But if you think for a minute that I am going to give in to the Hebrews and their god, then you can think again. For I am Pharaoh, King of all Egypt, and no one – no one in heaven and no one on earth – is going to tell me what to do!"

The magicians hurried away.

Pharaoh stood his ground.

And so the plagues continued.

Hail rained down on Pharaoh's fields and crushed all Egypt's crops. Then anything left growing was devoured by hungry locusts. Finally, darkness covered the whole of the land. And when the magicians had grown tired of bumping into the furniture and having nothing to eat, they took their empty stomachs and their skinned knees one last time into Pharaoh's palace.

They found him sitting... alone. He was no longer frustrated, no longer annoyed. No longer angry, no longer enraged. No, he just sat there, quietly brooding, with his teeth clenched tight and his knuckles white around the arm of his throne.

"What do you want?" he muttered, barely looking at his magicians.

"We want you to give up," urged the first magician.

"Please!" begged the second. "Please let the Hebrews go!"

"No one will think less of you," the first magician argued. "You have done all you could."

"But the Hebrew god is just too strong!" added the second. "And besides, we have heard. We have heard what the next plague will be."

Pharaoh slowly raised his eyes and stared at his magicians. "The death of the first born," he said softly. "Your son, and your son," he pointed. "And mine as well."

"Please, Your Majesty," the first magician pleaded. "My wife and I – we could not think of losing him!"

"We love our sons. And we know you love yours," the second magician continued. "And you have the power to save their lives!"

"Power?" sighed Pharaoh. "What power? The god of the Hebrews controls the wind and the rain and the light. But I am just a king. And yet. And yet..." And here the king smiled a hard and cruel smile. "And yet there is still one power that remains. The power to say 'No'."

"But the children," the magicians pleaded. "The children will die!"

The king's smile turned into a hard and cruel stare. "Sometimes," he answered coldly, "a leader has to harden his heart to the sufferings of his people for the sake of his people's good."

"For his people's good?" sighed the first magician.

"Or for the sake of his own pride?" muttered the second.

"Out!" Pharaoh commanded. "Get out!" he shouted again. "And if you want to keep your heads, you will never return to this place!"

One week later, the magicians stood solemnly together and stared out over the Red Sea.

"So he let them go, after all," the first magician sighed.

"The weeping. The wailing," sighed the second magician in return. "They say he tried hard to shut it out. But then his own son died – and that was too much, even for him."

"So he let them go. And then he changed his mind – again!"

"I suppose he thought he had them trapped. Perhaps it never occurred to him that a god who could send locusts and hail and turn the Nile to blood could quite easily divide a sea, as well."

"And so the Hebrews crossed on dry ground. And our own army? What about the soldiers sent after them?"

"Drowned. Drowned as they tried to follow. Drowned as the divided sea washed back over them."

"So our suffering was for…?"

"Nothing. Nothing at all."

"And what about Pharaoh?" asked the first magician. "What do you hear of him?"

The second magician shook his head. "One of his servants told me that he has forbidden anyone in the palace to even speak about this event. And he has ordered the court historians to make no record of it whatsoever."

"A proud man," muttered the first magician.

"Proud to the end," agreed the second.

And the two magicians turned away from the sea and walked sadly home.

Chapter Three

Retelling the Story

Find A Way "In"

If storytelling really is more a dialogue than a monologue, then someone has to get the conversation started. And that is why it is so important for the storyteller to decide how he or she is going to tell the story.

You mean you don't start with "once upon a time" and finish with "and they all lived happily ever after"? Not necessarily. In fact, one of the great challenges of storytelling is finding a way "in" to the story – that "hook", that "device", that "gimmick" if you like, that pulls the listener in and makes the experience memorable. Some of the people in the group may have heard your story before. This is particularly true with biblical storytelling, where preachers, Sunday school teachers and RE co-ordinators alike are faced with the annual task of finding an inventive way "in" to the Christmas and Easter narratives (not to mention Noah, Jonah, and David and Goliath). The last thing you want is to encounter that groaning, been-there-done-that look. And even if the story you are telling is new to the audience, it is still better to tell that story as creatively as possible – so they hear it at its best, the very first time.

So what do you do? You can start by just "playing around" with the story. Many years ago, I was asked to write a book about angels. The subject was all the rage at the time, and I didn't want to write a book that was just like all the rest. So I took a close look at the Bible stories about angels and asked a couple of questions: What if God created angels in the same way that he made us? Not white, winged clones, but unique individuals, suited to particular tasks. What if an angel's appearance had something to do with the job it was called to do? I tried to answer those questions in the book, and that is why, in *Angels, Angels All Around*, the angel who is sent to make a meal for Elijah in the desert bears a striking resemblance to a TV chef. The angel who leads Peter out of prison is a clever little Puck of a fellow. And the angel who rescues Daniel from the lions' den looks a bit like a lion himself and plays through the night with the beasts so their attention is diverted from their dinner! Was I reading between the lines? Certainly. But I believe that asking questions of the story is one means of finding a unique way into it.

Another way "in" is to alter the point of view from which the story is told. In my book, *Bible Baddies*, for example, I have retold familiar Bible stories from the point of view of the villains. The message of the story remains the same (and, in fact, sometimes becomes even clearer!), but the fresh approach really grabs an audience's attention. This works well with other kinds of stories too. In *The Wolf Who Cried Boy*, I simply reversed the roles of the traditional story. It's the wolf (a little wolf, in this case, who is fed up with his mother's cooking) who does the fibbing. And the boy (the promised treat to relieve the tedium of his mother's meals!) who provides the occasion for the lie! And in *The Three Billy Goats' Stuff*, I set the story in a school playground and made the troll the school bully. He was always threatening to beat up the smaller students, unless they gave him their "stuff", but thwarted, at last, by the three new "kids" in school. The possibilities are endless, and it can make a well-known story really riveting, once again, because the listeners are always wondering whether the ending will be same, and how you'll get there, having started from an unfamiliar place. And more than anything else, it's just good fun!

The trick is to surprise and to delight your listeners, because it's when they enjoying themselves that they are truly open to the power of the story itself. It's much as Aesop suggested in his fable about the sun and the wind – whimsy, humour, joy and delight are more effective paths to discovering truth and experiencing change than any heavy-handed approach. Granted, you will be called upon to tell stories that are, by their very nature, more serious. But even there, finding an original way "in" to the story, and surprising your audience, will open that story up – even to those who have heard it a hundred times before.

When it comes to Biblical storytelling, there is another good reason for finding an original and inspiring way "in" to the story. It makes the story shine anew for the teller, as well.

Several years ago, I was taking an RE class at the school across the street from the church I led. My remit was to talk with the class about the reasons Christians behave the way they do – how they decide what is right and what is wrong. I told them that Christians are people who follow Jesus. So they try to do the things he did. I asked them if they knew any good things that Jesus did.

One girl said that he healed people. A boy said that he fed people who were hungry. So we talked about the ways that we could do those things now. And then a little boy at the back put up his hand.

"Didn't Jesus die by being crushed under a big rock?" he asked.

I thought about that for a moment.

"No," I said. "He did die, but he didn't die that way." And then I explained how Jesus actually died.

"You might be thinking about what happened three days after he died," I continued. "Do you know what happened next?" I asked. And the little boy shook his head.

"Well," I went on, "When Jesus died, they buried him in a tomb, a grave, and rolled a big stone in front of it. And three days later, when the stone was rolled away, Jesus wasn't there any more. Jesus was alive."

The little boy looked at me, and I promise you, this is what he did. His mouth hung open and all he said was "Wow!"

I could have been the apostle Paul, in the first century, speaking to an audience in Corinth or Athens – because, just like those people, the boy had never heard that story. His reaction – wonder, amazement, awe – said it all.

That little boy is not alone. Our schools and communities and, sadly, yes, even our churches are filled with people who do not know The Story. Not that story, perhaps – but lots of other ones. And when they hear it, they are knocked out by it, excited, thrilled. One of my favourite retellings is the story of the stilling of the storm. And when I do it in schools, without fail, the audience gets dead quiet when Jesus stands up in the boat – and you can hear a pin drop when he tells the wind to "be quiet now" and the waves to "settle down". And it's all because almost no one knows what's going to happen next. And there's the disconnect. Because if you have been a Christian for a while and you are familiar with the story, then sometimes that "wonder" is missing. "Yes, of course, Jesus fed five thousand people and made the blind see and even raised the dead," you think, but the wonder – that initial amazement – is gone, or at least much diminished. This isn't a criticism, it's just what happens when anyone becomes familiar with a story (even an incredible one like the story of Jesus). It's easy to take it for granted.

The problem is that if you tell it in that been-there-done-that way, if the excitement isn't there for you, then it won't be there for those who hear the story either. And you will be doing both them and the story a disservice.

I always say that what Christians need to do is to rediscover the "shine" in the story – the thing that makes that story amazing for them. And the interesting thing is that the very process you use to rediscover the "shine" is the same process you use to retell a Bible story.

It begins with what may seem to you the most obvious, logical and sensible step. But it's a step that too often gets missed:

If you want to retell a story from the Bible, the first thing you need to do is to read it in the Bible.

See? Obvious! You'd think so, anyway. But the reality is that many people retell retellings, or work from a shaky and inexact memory, or just "wing it". And that just won't do. Not for retelling and particularly not for finding that shiny thing that makes it work for you.

I've been there myself, so I know what I'm talking about here. When I sat down to retell the story of the battle of Jericho for *The Lion Storyteller Bible*, I didn't look at the text at all. I figured I knew that story inside out. I went to Sunday school and Bible College and Seminary. Of course I knew the story of Jericho! And then I thought, well, maybe I should just have a peep – to make sure. And sure enough, when I actually read the text, I discovered something I'd never seen or heard before. An angel! An angel of the Lord, with a sword, encouraging Joshua on. Well, I got excited about that angel and stuck him in the story and he's been a unique part of that retelling ever since – a surprise to other people who thought they also knew all there was to know about that story.

Reading the text first gives you the chance to discover those interesting little details that will bring the story alive again for you. Sure, you can always use someone else's retelling. And as an author of loads of Bible retellings, it's in my interest that you do so. But I have to be honest with you too – the best retellings are the ones that spring from something interesting, exciting or novel that you yourself have found in the text.

The other reason for reading the text first is that it gives you the chance to ask questions of the text – questions your audience might well have and questions that you can find the answers to ahead of time. I do the same kind of preparation for a retelling as I would do for a sermon. If I stumble across something I don't understand, I consult a commentary or talk to someone who might know the answer. You can do the same. Talk to your pastor or priest. Ask for some good reference material. There is a lot of joy in that process and the discoveries that result from it. I was retelling the story of Jesus' first sermon in Nazareth, the one that's recorded in Luke 4. It's the one where the congregation seizes him at the end and tries to throw him off a cliff! I got to wondering about Nazareth – how big was it? How many people lived there? So I did a little research (OK, I googled it!) and it turns out that Nazareth had a population of only about 120 people at that time. One hundred and twenty, that's nothing! So most of those people would have known Jesus' family – no question. Which makes their reaction to his message even more extraordinary. This wasn't some stranger they were tossing into the valley – it was someone they knew, someone from their tiny little corner of the world – which made his claims even more ridiculous, blasphemous and audacious.

Or there's the parable of the friend who has a visitor at midnight. He doesn't have any food in his house, so he bangs on another friend's door until that friend relents and gives him some bread. It's Jesus' way of talking about persistence in prayer.

But did you ever wonder – what was that man doing, arriving at midnight? It's not as if there were lighted roads in those days. Wouldn't it have been dangerous? Well, no. I was in the Middle East a few years ago and had to catch a plane home at midnight. As we drove to the airport, we passed crowds of people on the road. In fact, we passed families having picnics. At midnight!

"Why are they out so late?" I asked my host.

And he looked at me as if I was stupid. "Because it's too hot to be out in the day!"

Makes sense, doesn't it? And it certainly helps to make sense of Jesus' story.

So start by reading the text. Then ask questions of the text. Oh, and if you're doing a Gospel story, read all three (or four) versions from the different Gospels. One version might suit your needs better than another.

When I read the passage from the Bible, there are three main elements I am looking for – the three elements that are a part of every story – character, setting and problem. Before we look more closely at those elements, the following stories show how I have looked for ways "in" to a couple of different passages.

Angel Food

Earlier in the chapter, I suggested that one way "in" to a story is to just play around with it, and gave *Angels, Angels All Around* as an example. This is one of my favourite stories from that book. (Let's face it – they are all my favourites – I love that book!) The premise, as I suggested earlier, is simple – God sends an angel to feed a prophet, so maybe that angel is a chef-type of angel, gifted particularly in the culinary arts. I suppose I had Delia Smith in mind, when I first wrote the book, but you can tell it any way you like – so if you want to Nigella-cize the angel, go for it! The story might read quite a bit differently, however!

Telling tips: *There aren't really any actions for this story, and its one you can tell on your own.*

Elijah was a pretty good prophet.

With God's help, he raised a boy from the dead. With God's help, he stopped the rain from falling, as a warning to Israel's evil King Ahab. And with God's help, he defeated the false priests of the even-more-evil Queen Jezebel.

So what was he doing sitting under a bush in the middle of the desert?

He was thinking about giving up, that's what.

He was tired – tired of fighting the evil in his land, and then seeing it all come back again. He was afraid – afraid that Queen Jezebel would carry out her threat to track him down and kill him. And he was worried – worried that even God would not be able to help him this time. Worried enough to run and hide in the desert.

And so Elijah prayed a prayer, a sad and tired and frustrated prayer. "Take me away, God," he prayed.

"Take my life before Jezebel does. Kill me now. I've had enough."

And then, with bush for his blanket and a desert stone for his pillow, Elijah fell into an exhausted sleep.

God heard Elijah's prayer. God understood Elijah's fear and frustration. So God answered Elijah.

Down the secret stair from heaven, where God's surprises are stored, came an angel. A very special angel. An angel who was more like your mother than your father. An angel who was more of a "she" than a "he".

The angel pulled back a branch of the bush that covered Elijah and let one or two sunbeams land on the prophet's sleeping face. "Poor tired thing," she whispered. And she gently shook her angel head. Then she let go of the branch and rubbed her big hands together as if she was ready to get to work.

The angel reached into one big apron pocket and pulled out a flat spoon. From her other pocket, she fetched a deep, wide, wooden bowl. She set these down beside the sleeping prophet and whispered softly in his ear, "Back in a minute, pet. I've got some shopping to do."

Then she threw herself into the sky and flew north, straight for the fertile lands along the Jordan River.

The angel stopped at a threshing floor and swept a pile of freshly harvested wheat into her apron pocket. Next, she swooped low over an orchard and snatched a branch, heavy with fresh fruit, from an olive tree. Finally, the angel soared high into the hills above the river and scooped a cup of fresh, cool water from a mountain stream. Then she sailed back to Elijah – without dropping a seed or spilling a drop.

The prophet turned and shook and mumbled in his sleep.

"Just rest now, my dear," the angel whispered. "It won't be long." And then she began to hum. (A hymn from Heaven's Throne Room? A ditty from Heaven's Kitchen? Or maybe they were one and the same.)

She hummed as she dumped the wheat – *kafloosh!* – onto a flat desert rock and ground it into flour. She hummed as she clutched the olives in her big hand and – *squooge!* – crushed the oil out of them. She hummed as she mixed the oil and the flour together in the bowl and – *bloop!* – added just one long drop of the mountain water.

And then she stopped humming. And stood up. And snapped her fingers.

Eggs!

She knew she'd forgotten something. Not even an angel can make a cake without eggs.

The angel wiped her hands on her apron and cocked her head, listening to the sounds of the desert. She heard the desert wind pick up bits of sand and send them scraping against desert stones. She heard tiny desert animals skitter and slither and skip across the desert floor.

And then she heard what she was listening for – the soft, chirping song of a desert bird. A partridge.

Quick as a bird herself, the angel chased the sound and found a nest. She whispered something to the partridge, who bowed and stepped aside. And the angel bent down and listened to the nest. In two of the eggs, she heard the flutter and scratch of young bird life. But two were silent and would never be more than eggs. Those she took, with a grateful nod to the mother. Then she flew back to Elijah.

The angel mixed in the eggs and whipped up the batter until it was rich and creamy and thick. And as a final touch, she reached into her pocket and pulled out a tiny bottle of... Something. (A spice from Heaven's Kitchen? A gift from Heaven's Throne Room? Or maybe they were one and the same.) She opened the bottle and sprinkled exactly seven golden flakes into the batter. Then she dipped one finger into the mix and tasted it to make sure it was just right.

Finally, she reached down deep into the hot desert sand. Down,

down, down – until she found a steaming hot rock at the bottom of a boiling underground stream. She grabbed hold of that rock and yanked it right out of the ground. Then she carved a hole out of the middle of the rock and poured her batter in. Right away it started to sizzle and bubble and bake.

In no time at all, the cake was done. The angel peeled away the rocky oven as if it were the skin of an orange. Then she set the hot cake and a cup of cold mountain water by Elijah's sleepy head.

She tapped him lightly on the shoulder. "Elijah," she whispered. "Elijah, it's time to wake up."

The last time Elijah had heard those words, they were on his mother's lips. And if his aching body hadn't told him he was lying on the ground in the middle of a desert, he would have sworn that he was back at home. So who woke him up? And what was that incredible smell?

Elijah's eyes snapped open and his questions were answered in a glance. In front of him were a freshly baked cake, a cup of cold water – and an angel!

"Go on," coaxed the smiling angel. "Try some. I made it just for you."

Elijah knew he should be afraid. But he wasn't. What he was – was hungry! He tore off a chunk of the cake and gobbled it down. It was heavenly! Rich, but not sickening. Moist but not soggy. Filling but not fattening. So delicious that Elijah had to help himself to another piece. And then another. He would have finished the whole cake if the angel hadn't started humming her little tune again, and if he hadn't stretched out, tummy full, and fallen asleep all over again. And not a restless sleep this time, but a long dreamy snooze.

Quietly the angel tidied up her utensils, tucking them one by one into her pockets. And when Elijah had slept long enough, she tapped him on the shoulder again.

"Wake up, Elijah. Finish your cake. You have a long trip ahead of you. You need all the strength you can get."

Again Elijah opened his eyes. The cake was still there. But this time the angel was gone. (Gone to Heaven's Throne Room? Back to Heaven's Kitchen? Or maybe they are one and the same.)

Elijah quickly finished off the cake, licking his fingers and picking up each crumb. When he was done, he was different. He was no longer tired. The sleep had refreshed him, and the cake had filled him up so he felt as if he could walk for forty days if he had to.

And, best of all, he was no longer worried and afraid. Let Jezebel come! Let Ahab do his worst! God would take care of his prophet. Elijah was sure of that now.

Then, at that very moment, Elijah stood up and set off for Mount Horeb, the holy mountain. He was going to meet God there. He was going to find out what God wanted him to do next. And he was going to thank God for answering his prayer in a way he'd never expected – with a cup of cold mountain water and angel food cake.

A Joke at Midnight

Here's another example from *Angels, Angels All Around*. When I tell this one, I make a big deal of the character voices – particularly the "pretend" old man. Ooh – and I've got a great song parody which you can have for free and that works a treat with this story. It's called "Help me, Rhoda" and is set to the tune of the Beach Boys' song, "Help Me, Rhonda".

Telling tips: *Again, there aren't really any actions for this story, and its one you can tell on your own*

Peter was asleep. His head thrown back, his mouth wide open. Singing a roaring, snoring song.

Peter was asleep, but he wasn't home in bed.

Peter was in prison. Peter the fisherman, the follower and friend of Jesus. There was a guard on his right and a guard on his left. And his arms were chained to the wall.

Peter was dreaming. He dreamed about King Herod who had shut him up in prison for talking about Jesus. King Herod, who was going to have him killed in the morning.

He dreamed about his friends, who were praying for him at that very moment, praying that he would be set free.

And then he dreamed another dream – a most unusual dream. Peter dreamed he saw a beam of light shoot into his cell, straight down from the ceiling to the floor. And an angel slid down that beam, like a boy shimmying down a tree. The angel was small and slim, no bigger than a boy. And he wore a wide mischievous grin – as if he was about to play some kind of enormous joke on someone.

Peter wanted to watch, but as so often happens in dreams, he fell back to sleep again. The next thing he knew, someone was thumping him on the side.

Those guards, he thought peevishly. Couldn't they let him have one last night's rest? He turned his head to the left and opened his eyes. The guard was asleep. He turned his head to the right. That guard was asleep too. Puzzled, he looked straight ahead. And there, not a hand's breadth from his face, was that mischievous grin he'd seen in his dream.

Was Peter dreaming, now? He couldn't tell.

The angel wrapped his small hands around two of Peter's fat fisherman's fingers and jumped back, pulling Peter to his feet. Then the angel skipped away a few steps and motioned for Peter to shake his hands.

This has got to be a dream, thought Peter. But he shook his hands, like the angel showed him. And his chains fell off!

Quick as a child, the angel leaped to catch them before they rattled to the floor. Then he gently set them down, grinning and giggling all the while.

Peter grinned too. What a dream this is! he thought.

Suddenly, from out of nowhere, Peter's clothes came flying across the cell and hit him smack in the face.

"Put them on," a small voice giggled.

Peter put them on. And just as he'd finished, his sandals dropped lightly – one, two – in front of his feet.

"These, too," the voice giggled again. "It's time to go."

Peter looked at the angel. He looked at the sleeping guards. He looked at the empty chains. A wonderful dream, indeed! he thought.

The angel slipped through the bars of the cell door and motioned for Peter to follow. Peter tried to slip through, but his full fisherman's figure got in the way.

Chuckling, the angel reached up and snapped out two of the metal bars.

Peter sucked in his belly and tried again. Finally, with a shove and a grunt, he burst through.

He started down the hall and then remembered with a shock that two guards were always stationed outside his cell. Peter stopped and turned around slowly. He wondered for a moment if this dream would turn into a nightmare.

The guards were still there all right. Standing to attention. But their eyes stared blindly ahead. And in their hands, where their spears should have been, the angel was placing the iron bars he had snapped from the cell door.

The angel stood between them, his arms crossed and his head tossed back, laughing a laugh that Peter might have called "naughty", had he not known it came from heaven.

"An amazing dream!" said Peter.

The angel slipped past him and headed down a long hall towards the prison gates, waving for Peter to follow. Together they crept, the tiny bright angel, toes barely touching the floor, and his dark-cloaked shadow, lumbering behind on flat fisherman's feet.

As they approached the first gate, the angel whispered into Peter's ear, "Do you like to play make-believe?"

Make-believe? When Peter was a small boy – smaller even than this angel – he used to pretend that he was with his father out on the sea. He'd drag a piece of old net across the beach and haul in catches of flat stone "fish".

"Sure," Peter whispered. He liked to play make-believe.

"Good," said the angel. "You can pretend to be Amos, the old man who cleans out the cells. It should get us past the next guards."

"But I don't look anything like him," Peter protested. "And I don't sound anything like him. What will I do if they ask me a question?"

"Just stoop over," ordered the little angel, "and put your hand on your back, as if it's sore. Now walk very slowly, as if you're afraid of falling down."

The angel pulled Peter's cloak over his head, making a hood to hide his face. "That's good. That's very good," he sniggered. "And don't worry about how you'll sound. Leave the talking to me."

Peter stooped and shuffled his way to the first gate.

But when he saw the guards, he wondered if it wasn't time to pinch himself and wake up from this dream.

Too late! A voice was already echoing out from somewhere inside his cloak. "Evening boys," it quivered. "Another late night and – oh! – my back is killing me.

"'Old Amos,' my wife says, 'you're too old to be scrubbing out those cells. Think of your rheumatism. Think of your legs. Think of the diseases you could pick up in that place!'

"'Ah, but old Agatha,' I says back, 'the king needs me. The prisoners need me. Those guards – those brave young boys – they need me. And they're always so kind to me,' I says, 'very kind, indeed.'"

One of the guards swung open the gate, and the other chuckled and reached into his belt. "Here you go, old man," he said. And he tossed Peter a small coin.

Peter started to reach out and catch it, but the angel quietly slapped his hand and whispered, "No, let it drop. Now stoop to pick it up, but watch out for the guard's..."

BOOT! The guard's foot found Peter's behind and sent him sprawling.

The angel made small clucking noises inside Peter's cloak. "Tsk! Tsk! You boys will have your fun."

Peter climbed slowly and shakily to his feet. Then, chased by the guards' laughter, he skittered down the hall like an old spider.

"Never mind them," grinned the angel. "We'll have the last laugh."

By the time they reached the main gate, the one that led out of the prison and into the city, Peter was really enjoying his dream. The gate was massive, so there was no need for any guards. Who could possibly break out of it? And who would want to break in?

Peter looked down at the angel and smiled. "Now what?" he said. "Let me guess. You just wave your hand and the gates swing open, right?"

The angel smiled back. "You're catching on." And with a giggle, he waved his hand. The gate swung open.

Together they walked through dark, deserted streets towards the house where Peter's friends were praying.

And they filled those silent streets with laughter.

They sniggered as they imagined how those guards would feel when they woke up.

They cheered when they thought about the reaction of Peter's worried friends.

And they snorted and guffawed as they pictured the look on Herod's face when he heard the news.

"This has been great fun," said the angel as they reached the house of Peter's friends. "But now it's time for me to go."

"And time for me to wake up, I suppose," Peter sighed.

"No," the angel giggled as a beam of light shot down from the stars. "That's the best joke of all. You've been awake the whole time!" And with a snap of his fingers, he slid up the beam and out of sight.

Peter stood there for a moment staring up into the sky. A cool breeze ruffled his hair and sent a shiver down his spine. He looked around. The street was empty.

Then he reached out and touched the solid stone wall of his friends' house. He rapped his knuckles against their hard wooden door. And he listened to the astonished voice of the young girl who answered it.

"It's Peter!" she gasped. "It's Peter! He's free!" And she ran inside to tell the others, leaving Peter standing outside.

So it was true. And not a dream at all. The guards. The broken bars. The angel.

Peter shook his head. He had escaped. He could hardly believe it. What a night! What a rescue! What a joke!

Then a smile found its way onto his free fisherman's face. And he stepped inside to share the joke with his friends.

Help Me, Rhoda

Peter was in prison but an angel came to set him free
His friends were all at Mark's house, praying for his liberty
Peter showed up at the door
He knocked until his knuckles were sore!
And he cried out,
"Help me, Rhoda! Help me, I just got outta jail!"

Chorus:
"Help me, Rhoda, help, help me Rhoda (x6)
Help me, Rhoda, please, I just got outta jail!"

Rhoda told the others, but they thought that she was off her tree
"The meeting's almost over and we're ready for a cup of tea!"
"Rhoda, you're mad!" they said.
"Poor Peter is probably dead."
But he cried out,
"Help me, Rhoda! Help me, I just got outta jail!"

Chorus

Rhoda was persistent. "Peter's out there; you must trust my word!"
"I may just be your servant, but I know exactly what I heard!"
They gave in and opened the door.
And stared in shock at what they saw…
It was Peter crying,
"Help me, Rhoda! Help me, I just got outta jail!"

Chorus

Who are the Characters?

Who are the main characters in this story? That's the first question you want to ask. As I suggested earlier, an audience's identification with the characters can help to draw the group into that story. So you need to bring the characters to life. And to do that, you need to understand who they are. When retelling a Bible story, it is important that you are faithful to what we know *from* the Bible about the characters from the text. When I retold David and Goliath in *The Lion Storyteller Bible*, I saw it in terms of "little", "bigger" and "big". Who are the three main characters, after all? David, who is little. King Saul, who is bigger. And Goliath, who is very big indeed! This very simple device not only gave me a way to describe the characters, it also helped to state the problem.

But there is more to these characters than just their size, isn't there? So you take some time to think about them – not as cardboard cut-outs, but as real people. Who are they, really? What adjectives might I use to describe them?

David is not only small; he is brave. He has a deep trust in God, because he has seen God help him in the past. The jealousy that eventually destroys Saul is perhaps not yet fully realized. But there is already a stubborn streak to his nature, perhaps brought on by a deep sense of insecurity. He is, after all, in Samuel's eyes at least, only king by God's sufferance. King by default. And Goliath? Well, when I told this story from Goliath's point of view in *More Bible Baddies*, I imagined that he was one of those people who was always bigger than everyone around him – even as a child. And that he was always being told off: "Don't break those toys, Goliath! Be careful with your sister. Don't squeeze that kitty so hard!"

So, in the end, he grows up hating little things. And then, of course, I can have that ironic moment at the end of the story, with the stone hurtling towards his head, and make the point that that little thing is the last thing he ever sees!

If you take the time to do this with every story you retell, you will get used to finding those traits that bring your characters to life. Is there a subjective element in this? Sure. Like I said, it's important to be faithful to what the text tells us, but beyond that we inevitably see the characters in a story from our own perspective – and that helps to give them life, as well. I do this "find the adjective to describe the character" exercise whenever I train storytellers, and it's fascinating to see the different ways that people respond to and describe characters, based largely on their own experiences. Some people see nothing but irresponsibility, ingratitude and wastefulness in the character of the prodigal son. Others see his rebellion more as a result of curiosity, or restlessness or a desire to define himself in his own right. It doesn't take a psychologist to work out that that there is a certain amount of personal experience behind those interpretations!

Sometimes it also helps to invent a character. Not out of thin air, obviously, but drawn perhaps from a crowd that is in the story anyway. Why? Because sometimes, you need a perspective from someone other than one of the main characters to understand what the story is about. Here's an example:

In the gospel story when a man's friends lower him through the roof, there are two problems. There is the man's need to get to Jesus – which his friends solve by tearing up their neighbour's roof so that their friend can be healed. But there is also the theological controversy that erupts between Jesus and the religious leaders when Jesus tells the man that his sins are forgiven. When I retold this story in *The Lion Storyteller Bible*, I suppose that I could simply have ignored the second problem. The difficulty, though, is that the two problems are very closely connected – Jesus heals the man to demonstrate that he has the authority to forgive his sins. The solution I came up with was to create a character – the daughter of one of the religious leaders – to serve as a set of eyes for the reader. She was then able to look objectively at the situation as it developed, and also ask the kinds of questions that any child might: why is someone tearing a hole in the roof? Will Jesus be able to help the man? Why is my father so angry at what Jesus is saying? In a sense, the main problem becomes: what's going on here? But the other problems get solved along the way, and the reader/listener is given someone specific to whom they can relate. And best of all, the original intention of the story is preserved.

I think that being faithful to the original story is incredibly important when it comes to biblical storytelling. We can invent new characters, insert new details, ask questions of the text and fill in some of the gaps between the lines. But it is critical that we are faithful to what we understand to be the intent of that particular story. And it is also critical, I think, that we are faithful to the facts that we have already been given. I will readily admit that some of the gaps I have tried to "fill in" have been pretty wide. And I have had plenty of conversations with people who were not comfortable with that. My response was that they should work to their own comfort level as far as gaps in the story are concerned. Some storytellers will not want to stray from the text at all. That's fine. But I also think there is room for some "sanctified imagining" between the gaps, particularly if that creativity helps to open up the story for others.

But what if your listeners go back to the Bible and they discover that the story isn't just like you told it? That's quite possible, so I suggest that you are always honest about what you're doing. In the preface to *Angels, Angels All Around* (my most "gappy" book by far!) I tried to make clear exactly what I was doing and why. And I preface those stories in the same way when I tell them.

"Here's the story of Daniel in the Lions' Den," I say. "You may have heard it before, but I'm going to tell it in a different way. I'm going to glue it together with that game you might have played – What's the Time, Mr Wolf? – and we're going to see what happens!"

The only story that I can honestly say has violated these principles is my retelling of the story of Ehud and King Eglon in *Bible Baddies*. At the time I wrote the story, I was struggling with some of the more violent parts of the Old Testament and effectively developed a story around the story of Ehud to explore the repercussions of that violence. Again, I explained what I was doing in the introduction to the story, and admit the same thing whenever I tell it. But, looking back on it, this story is probably now on the edge of my comfort zone, as well!

Ehud and Eglon

Right then, this is the story where my "gap management" may well have gone astray. I'll leave it to you to decide.

Telling tips: *Like the rest of the former* Bible Baddies *pieces, this one needs to be read or told dramatically.*

Every night it was the same. For eighteen years, the same. Ehud would wake up, suddenly, cold and sweating and afraid. And that face, the face in the dream, would be laughing at him all over again.

Shouting, that's how the dream began.

"The Moabites are coming! They've crossed the river and they're heading towards the village!"

What followed next was a mad, rushing blur – a spinning haze of colour and fear and sound. His father's hand. His sister's screams. His mother's long black hair. Goats and pots and tables, running and flying and falling down.

And then, suddenly, everything would slow down again, to half its normal speed. And that's when the man would appear. The laughing man. The fat man. Eglon, king of Moab.

He would climb down from his horse, every bit of his big body wobbling. And with his soldiers all around, hacking and slicing and kicking and killing, he would walk up to Ehud's family, each step beating in time with the little boy's heart.

His father, Gera, would fall to his knees. His mother, as well, with his sister in her arms. And then the big man, laughing still, would raise his sword and plunge it first into his father, and then through his mother and his sister too.

Finally, the laughing man would raise his bloodied sword and turn to five-year-old Ehud. But before the king could strike, there would come a sound, a call, from somewhere off in the distance. The king would turn his head, look away for just a second, and Ehud would start to run – run between the burning buildings, run past his dying neighbours, run till the nightmare was over, run... until he awoke.

Every night, for eighteen years – that's how long the dream had followed Ehud. But tonight, he promised himself, tonight the dream would come to an end. For today, King Eglon of Moab, the fat man, the laughing man, the man who had murdered his family, would come to an end, as well.

Ehud thanked God for his family, and particularly for his father, and for the gift that his father had passed on to him. It was a gift that not even the Moabites could take away, a gift that made him the perfect candidate for the job he was about to do – the gift of a good left hand.

Most soldiers were right-handed. They wore their swords hanging from the left side of the body, and then reached across the body to draw them from their sheaths. That was what the enemy looked for; that's what the enemy watched – the right hand. For the slightest twitch, the smallest movement of that hand might signal that a fight was about to begin. So, a left-handed man enjoyed a certain advantage, particularly if his sword was hidden.

Ehud rubbed his eyes, rolled off his sleeping mat and reached for his sword – the special sword that he had designed just for this mission.

It was only eighteen inches long – far too short for battle, but just the right size for strapping to his thigh and hiding under his robes. And it was sharpened on two edges, so he could cut in both directions. He'd wipe the smile from the fat man's face, all right!

He'd waited for this day for eighteen years. And for those same eighteen years, the nation of Israel had been paying tribute to King Eglon. For the invasion which had destroyed Ehud's village had also swept across the land and resulted in Israel's surrender to Moab. And so, every year, great quantities of treasure and produce and livestock had to be delivered to the royal palace and presented to Eglon himself, as a sign of Israel's submission.

Today was the day – Tribute Day. And the man chosen to lead Israel's procession, chosen by God himself to walk right into the presence of the king, was none other than Ehud, the left-handed man, the man with the sword strapped to his thigh, the man who was finally in a position to set both himself and his people free.

Ehud thought he would be nervous, but instead he was overcome with a sense of calm and purpose. He led the procession, according to plan, out of Israel and across the Jordan River, past the stone statues of Gilgal and into the palace of the king.

He had imagined this moment for years – face to face, finally, with the man he hated most in all the world. What will I feel? he had often wondered. Hatred? Disgust? The overwhelming urge to reach out and strike Eglon where he stood? All those feelings, he knew, he had to overcome if the plan was to succeed. He must be submissive, polite and reverential if he was to win the trust of this tyrant. But when Eglon, at last, appeared, Ehud was shocked by what he actually felt.

The king was still a big man – now far heavier than Ehud had remembered. So heavy, in fact, that his attendants had to help support his weight as he staggered towards his throne. But as for laughter, there was none at all, not even a chuckle – just a hard and constant wheeze as the man struggled to move.

Pity. That's what Ehud felt. And he couldn't believe it. Pity, and the surprising sense that, somehow, he had been robbed. This was not the man he'd dreamed of – the fat man, the laughing man, the nightmare man. No, this was a sad and pathetic man, crippled by excess and by power, and unable to raise a sword even if he had wanted to.

Still, Ehud reminded himself, there was the mission – the job he believed God had sent him to do. And pity or not, for the sake of his people, he would do it.

And so he bowed and he scraped and he uttered the obligatory words:

"Noble Potentate, Ruler of all you survey, Great and Mighty One."

Then he stepped aside as, one by one, the gifts were laid before the king. Eglon, however, hardly paid attention. He nodded, almost imperceptibly, and acknowledged each part of the tribute with the slightest wave of his hand. It looked to Ehud as if he was bored with the whole affair, or just too old and tired to care.

When the formalities had finished, Ehud sent his entourage away, then turned to the king and said, "I have a secret message for you, Your Majesty."

For the first time, Eglon looked interested. His dull eyes showed some spark of life as they focused on Ehud.

"Silence!" the king wheezed at his attendants. "This man has something to tell me."

Ehud looked around, nervously. "It's for your ears only," he whispered. "Perhaps if we could meet somewhere... alone?"

The king considered this, and then nodded. "Very well," he agreed. "Meet me upstairs, in my roof chamber. It's cooler there, anyway. Oh," and here he glanced at the sword that hung from Ehud's side, the long sword, the decoy sword, "you will, of course, leave your weapon outside."

Ehud smiled and bowed, "Of course!"

That smile never left Ehud's face – not once, while he waited for the king to be helped up to his chamber. For the plan was working perfectly, as all the spies had said it would.

Eglon loved secrets, they had assured him. Dealing and double-dealing, they explained, were how he had hung on to his throne. And that made this plan all the more sweet. For Ehud's robe concealed a secret that the king would never expect!

Finally, the guards called Ehud up to the roof chamber. They looked at him suspiciously. They took away the sword that hung at his side. Then they sent him in to the king.

Ehud bowed again. And the king waved him forward.

"So who is this message from?" asked Eglon, and the cruelly calculating look in his eyes reminded Ehud, at last, of the man he saw each night in his dreams.

"From one of your commanders?" the king continued.

"Or from one of your spies?" he went on.

"Or perhaps the sight of all that treasure has convinced you to speak for yourself – to betray your own people?" And with that, the king began to laugh. A little, choked and wheezing laugh, but it was enough – enough to rekindle Ehud's ebbing wrath, enough to force him to play his secret hand.

"No," he answered firmly. "The message is neither mine nor my commander's. The message I have for you is from God himself." And he reached his left hand under his robe and drew his sword.

Three times – that is how he had always planned it. Once for his father, once for his mother, once for his poor murdered sister. But the first blow was so fierce that the sword plunged all the way in, swallowed up past its hilt in the fatty folds of Eglon's stomach. And even though Ehud tried to retrieve it, all he got was a fistful of entrails and blood.

Ehud locked the chamber doors to buy himself some time; then he hurried out down the servants' staircase. A part of him wanted to savour this moment – to stand and gloat over Eglon's bloated corpse. But if he was to avoid a similar fate, he needed to run. And he thanked God for the escape route the spies had plotted out for him.

Down from the roof chamber and along the quiet corridors of the private quarters – that was the plan. And, sure enough, he passed no one but a startled maid. He rehearsed it as he went: one more turn, one more hallway and he would be out. But as he dashed around the final corner, he stumbled over something, and fell in a sprawling heap onto the floor.

It was a boy. A little boy. "And he's not hurt," thought Ehud, relieved.

"Who are you?" the little boy asked, as he picked himself up and flashed a friendly smile.

"I'm… umm… it's not important," Ehud stammered. "I have to be going."

"Well, if you see my grandfather," the boy said, "will you tell him I'm looking for him? He said he would tell me a story."

"Your grandfather?" asked Ehud.

"The king, silly!" the little boy grinned. "Everybody knows that!" And Ehud just stood there, frozen.

He could hear the chamber doors crashing down. He could hear the shouts of the attendants, and their cries, "The king, the king is dead! Someone has murdered the king!"

He had to go. He had so little time. But all he could do was stand there. And look at the boy. And look at his own bloodied hand. And look at the boy again. And watch as the smile evaporated from his innocent five-year-old face.

And then Ehud ran. Ran as he ran in his dream. Out of the palace and past the stone statues to the hills of Seirah. The army of Israel was waiting there – waiting for his return. And as soon as he shouted, "King Eglon is dead!" the army swooped down to the valley below.

Ten thousand died that day. Moab was defeated. Israel was freed. And Ehud had his revenge, at last. And finally, after much carousing and shouting and celebrating, he rolled, exhausted, onto his mat, looking forward to his first full night's sleep in eighteen years.

But unlike Ehud's enemies, the dream would not be so easily defeated. For as the night wore on, it returned – more real than ever.

There was the little boy. There was the shouting. There was the slashing and the screaming and the dying. Ehud trembled and shook just as he had for eighteen years. But when he looked, at last, into the eyes of the man with the bloodied sword, Ehud awoke with a start. For the man with the sword was left-handed. And the killer's face was his own.

Down Through the Roof

As I said earlier in this chapter, sometimes it helps to create a character for the sake of the story itself. To be fair, I suppose that the little girl appears in this retelling to help the reader/hearer understand the point of the story. But given the fact that we are two thousand years down the line from the culture in which Jesus lived, it's useful to have a kind of cultural guide to lead us through the story, and to lead us in a way that's (hopefully) not clunky or too obvious.

Telling tips: *Ask the group to pretend to be Anna with you. Poke your fingers through the hole in her pretend skirt, pretend to squeeze through the hole in the crowd, look up through the hole in the roof together, and try not to giggle (hands over mouths) when Jesus asks his very important question. Then, at the end, look up through the hole in the roof again.*

Anna stuck a finger through the hole in her skirt.

"How did that get there?" she wondered.

She would have run to her mother to have it mended, but her mother was on the other side of the house. And the house was full.

Packed full.

Jammed full.

Chock-a-block full.

Why? Because Jesus was visiting.

The old man and woman standing in front of Anna shifted, and she squeezed into the hole between them. She could see better now.

Jesus was a lot like her father. They both taught people about God. They both prayed beautiful prayers. But Jesus could do something else. Something her father had never done. Jesus could make sick people well! No wonder the whole town had crowded into her house.

Suddenly something dropped on Anna's head.

Anna looked up. And there was another hole – a hole in the roof!

Anna stepped back.

The hole got bigger.

The crowd stepped back.

And the hole got bigger still.

"What's going on up there?" shouted Anna's father. And, instead of an answer, a man dropped through the hole. A man lying on a mat with a rope at each corner. A poor, sick man who could not even move. His friends lowered him carefully to the floor, and Jesus gently laid a hand on his head.

"My friend," Jesus said, "the wrong things you have done are now forgiven."

"Wait a minute!" growled Anna's father. "Wait just a minute. Only God can take away someone's sins. Just who do you think you are?"

Oh dear, thought Anna. Her father often got angry when he talked with people about God.

But Jesus wasn't angry at all. "Which is easier," he said calmly, "to forgive a lame man's sins, or to make him walk?"

It was all Anna could do not to giggle. What a silly question, she thought. One is just as hard as the other!

"Well," Jesus continued. "To show you that God has given me the power to fix what is wrong in this man's heart, I shall fix what is wrong with his legs."

"Stand up!" Jesus ordered the man. "You can do it."

And the man did!

What is more, he rolled up the mat, slung it over his shoulder and walked out through the front door.

His friends climbed down from the roof to join him. The crowd followed behind, cheering. But all Anna could do was stare up through that hole and smile!

Goliath

This retelling first appeared in *More Bible Baddies*. And it's here largely because I think I probably got the imaginative gap stuff right in this case. I love this retelling and hope you will, too.

Telling tips: *Once again – read it or tell it with lots of drama. A big growly voice will definitely help (see Chapter 4 on tips and techniques).*

He hated little things. And maybe that was because he had never really been little himself.

He'd been a baby, once, of course. But he was the biggest baby the people of Gath had ever seen! So it was big robes and big sandals and big toys, right from the start. And "Don't push that little boy, dear". And "Careful with that pot, child". And "Don't squeeze the kitty so hard, Goliath – you'll hurt him".

Little kitties. Little puppies. Little people. The world was full of them! And it didn't take long for them to notice that he was different – and to bring it, constantly, to his attention.

Some children return teasing with humour. Others with sullen stares. But Goliath chose fear. Even the most harmless comment about his size would result in a furious beating from the big boy. Yes, he was beaten a few times by some of Gath's older lads. But he soon outgrew them all, and then no one dared challenge the boy who stood nearly seven feet tall!

His chosen occupation was chosen for him.

"There's only one thing to do with bullies," he overheard his father say. "The army! That'll sort him out."

Given his size and his strength, he might have risen high in the ranks. But his obvious hatred for "the little generals" and "their little rules" kept him marching with the infantry. In the end, there was only one thing he was good for – frightening the enemy. And Goliath was very good at that, indeed!

He'd strap on his armour – all one hundred and twenty gleaming pounds of it.

Then he'd pick up his spear – ten feet long, with a ten pound iron point.

And finally he would stand at the front of the Philistine troops – a shining colossus of a man.

"A challenge!" he would roar – roar across the valley to whatever army was camped on the other side. "A challenge is what I offer! Send your best man to fight me. And if he wins (and here Goliath always had a little chuckle), we shall be your slaves."

A few men had taken up his challenge. Little men. With little swords. And Goliath always smiled when he remembered how he had crushed their little heads and left their little bodies broken and twisted and torn.

Most men, however, never even tried. His presence alone made their little hearts beat with fear and sent them retreating to their little tents.

He expected as much today. The Israelites were not just a little people, they were the littlest of them all! A few scattered tribes. A puny, ramshackle army. And if what he had heard was true – just one little god to protect them. It hardly seemed worth the trouble, but he marched out anyway, into the valley of Elah, and issued his customary challenge. He anticipated a short day's work. But he had no idea how short it would turn out to be.

The Israelites heard the challenge, as they had every day for the past forty days. And, to a man, they trembled. But someone else heard the challenge too. Someone who had never heard it before. And it made him angry.

Maybe it had to do with his feelings about his people. Maybe it had to do with his feelings about his God. Or maybe he was just tired of being little.

He was the youngest of eight brothers, after all. And no matter how much courage he had shown defending his father's flock of sheep, they all still thought of him as the "runt". Hand-me-down sandals and pass-me-down robes – that was his lot. And while his older brothers got to serve as soldiers, the best he could do was bring them lunch, and carry chunks of goat cheese to their commanders!

"If only," David dreamed, "I could do something big, for a change."

And then he heard Goliath's challenge.

"So what do you get if you beat the giant?" he said to a soldier close by.

"A king's ransom," the soldier answered. "The king's daughter, too. Oh, and a terrific tax break for you and your family."

"Well," mused David, "I'm surprised someone hasn't accepted the challenge already."

And that's when he felt a hand – a big hand – on his shoulder. The hand belonged to his oldest brother, Eliab.

"So what are you doing here?" Eliab growled.

"Bread... umm, cheese," David muttered.

"Excuses, more like it," Eliab growled again. "Get back to the fields, where you belong!"

But David did not go back to the fields. No, he crept along the front lines, talking to one soldier after another, always about the giant. Finally, word got back to King Saul, who asked to see the boy.

The giant, meanwhile, was still waiting.

"Their little hearts are in their little throats," he chuckled, in a nasty sort of way. Then he looked down at his shield-bearer. The little man was not chuckling back. In fact, it was all he could do, in the hot noonday sun, to keep himself and the shield standing upright.

"Pathetic," Goliath muttered, and then wondered if the Israelites would ever send him a challenger.

"So you want to fight the giant?" grinned King Saul.

David had seen that look before. He got it from his big brothers, all the time. It was that "I'm-not-taking-you-seriously", "You're-just-a-little-shepherd-boy" kind of look.

So David stood as tall as he could and answered with the straightest face and the deepest voice he could manage.

"Yes, Your Majesty. I do."

"And what makes you think you can beat him?" the king continued.

David didn't even have to think.

"I have fought lions," he said. "And I have fought bears. All to save my father's sheep. And, every time, the Lord God has helped me win. I am sure he will do the same with this giant."

The king didn't know what to do. The boy had courage. The boy had faith. But if he allowed him to fight the giant, the boy would also soon be dead! Still, he needed a champion – any champion! So he made the boy an offer.

"My armour," said the king, pointing to the other side of the tent. "At least, take my armour. My shield. My sword. My breastplate. Whatever you like! You will need all the protection you can get."

David looked at the armour. He even tried a piece or two of it on. But it was much too big and much too heavy for him.

"I have all the protection I need," he said to the king, at last. "The Lord God himself will be my breastplate. He, alone, will be my shield." And he bowed and he turned, and he walked out of the tent.

Goliath, meanwhile, was tapping one big toe on the ground and humming an old Philistine folk song.

"In another minute, we're going back to camp," he said to his shield-bearer, who breathed a relieved sigh and thanked every Philistine god he could think of. But before he could finish his prayer, a cheer rang out from the Israelite camp. Someone was walking onto the battlefield.

"At last!" Goliath drooled, like a hungry man who has just been called for dinner.

The figure looked small, at first. Goliath chalked it up to the distance. But the closer he got, the smaller he seemed, until the giant realized, at last, that his challenger was no more than a boy!

"Is this some kind of joke?" he muttered to his shield-bearer. But neither the shield-bearer nor the boy were laughing.

"Or is it…" and here the giant's words turned into a snarl, "is it some kind of Israelite insult? Do they mock me? Do they make fun of me? Well, we'll see who has the last laugh!"

And then he roared – roared so the ground shook, and the shield-bearer, as well.

"Do you think I am a dog?" he roared. "That you come at me with this little stick of a boy? Send me a real challenger. Or surrender!"

"I am the real challenger," said David, in that deep voice he had used before the king. "And," (here his voice broke) "the God I serve is the real God too. And he will give me the victory this day!"

Goliath had heard enough. He grabbed his shield and raised his spear and charged. Little people and little generals and little soldiers. Little things had plagued him all his life! And now this little boy and his little army and his pathetic little god were going to pay. He'd skewer the lad and crush his little head and show them all what someone big and strong could do!

But as he rushed, enraged, towards the boy, David calmly reached into his shepherd's pouch. He placed a small stone in his sling, and he swung it round his head. Then he prayed that God would make his throw both strong and true.

The stone and the giant sped towards each other. And, at the last moment, Goliath caught a glimpse of it – a tiny speck, a minute fragment, so small it was hardly worth avoiding. But when it struck him between the eyes, he roared and he cried and he fell crashing to the ground. And that little thing was the last thing that the giant ever saw!

Jars

One of the tricks of any retelling is the choice of "point of view". In this case, I didn't invent the children – they were already there. But I did name them, flesh them out and give them a lot more to do, largely because I thought that seeing much of the story from their perspective would help draw other children in. And also because the wonder of the miracle – following all the hard work of the gathering and dropping of jars, simply seemed more wonderful – more miraculous – when seen through their eyes. Finally, I think that taking the time to make them real people in a real family makes the miracle and their rescue more meaningful.

Telling tips: *There are no special tips for telling this one – unless you have lots of children in front of you, lots of jars, and a "bottomless" jug of oil – to demonstrate.*

Daniel peeped out of the window. He was only six, and just tall enough to stand on his tiptoes and stick his nose up over the sill.

His little brother, David, was only four, and he wanted to see, as well. So he pulled a stool to his brother's side and, rocking back and forth as he went, clambered up on it.

"Watch out!" Daniel complained.

"But I want to see too!" moaned David. "I want to see Mum!" And he stuck his nose over the sill, as well, with a "What's she doing?"

"She's talking to that man," explained Daniel. "She said his name is Elisha. He's a prophet – like Dad was."

"What are they saying?" asked David.

"Can't tell." Daniel shrugged. "Too far away."

And so they were. In fact, as Daniel and David's mother had planned, they were just close enough so the boys could keep an eye on her, and just far enough away so they could not hear what she was saying.

"Nathan had debts," she sighed, wiping a tear away with her sleeve.

And the prophet nodded, like he knew.

"The thing is..." she continued, and it was all she could do to keep from bursting into tears. "The thing is, now that he is dead, his creditors want to collect what he owed from me."

"And?" asked Elisha.

"And," she sighed even harder. "I have nothing to give them. Nothing at all. So they have told me that they will take the boys and sell them into slavery to pay the debt."

Now Elisha sighed, looking past the desperate mother to the two clumps of curly black hair that kept bobbing up and down at the bottom of her window.

"Do they know?" he whispered.

She shook her head. "No, of course not. How could I tell them? They just know things are bad. We have so little to eat. They miss their father."

"So there's literally nothing left?" asked the prophet.

"A bit of oil." The woman shrugged. "That's all."

"Oil, you say?" The prophet grinned. "The sign of God's presence." And then he nodded. "That will do nicely."

"I told you to stop rocking!" Daniel shouted. "I told you you'd fall down!"

"I'm OK," grunted David, picking himself up off the floor and rubbing one elbow.

"But you broke the stool!" Daniel shouted again. "Mum is going to be really angry!"

And just at that moment, she burst back into the house.

"Boys!" she announced. "I've got something for you do. Now!"

"David broke the stool!" shouted Daniel.

And David started to cry.

"It's all right," she said, giving him a hug. "Really. There's something very important I need you to do. And you have to do it quickly."

"What is it?" asked David.

"You have to borrow jars," she said. "Empty jars. As many as you can get. From everyone in the village."

"But why?" asked Daniel.

"Because Elisha said so," she nodded. "Now, go!"

So they went – one brother up the street and the other down, banging on doors, borrowing jars, and juggling them in their arms all the way back home.

David dropped a couple on the way. And Daniel sighed and shook his head. But, several trips later, when they had begged and bothered and pestered every neighbour, their house was filled with jars.

David and Daniel's mum shut the door.

"It's what the prophet said to do," she explained. Then she took what little oil she had and poured it into one of the jars. She poured and she poured, until the jar filled up.

"I don't get it," said Daniel. "There wasn't enough oil to do that."

"I know," said his mum. "But the prophet told me to keep on pouring."

So she did. And before they knew it, the second jar was full! And the one after that!

"This is fun!" chirrupped David, replacing the full jar with an empty one. "Let's see if we can fill them all."

And, believe it or not, they did! One by one, they filled every jar in that house. The jars on the floor and on the chairs and on the table: the jars in the corner of the floor and the middle of the floor. Every jar everywhere!

"What do we do now?" asked Daniel, tiptoeing round the jars.

"We sell what we can and we keep what's left for ourselves," answered his mum. "That's what the prophet said. And I think that should be enough to pay all our debts and take care of us for a long time."

"And to buy a new stool?" asked David sheepishly.

"Maybe even two," his mother grinned.

And she hugged them both and held them tight.

"One for each of my boys."

Question Time

This illustrates telling the story from the perspective of a key character. Telling it from Peter's viewpoint is another example of the way that understanding the part a character plays in a story can help you to decide how to tell it. There is a lot of background detail that helps to make this story clear to the hearer – the nature of the temple tax, Peter's recent confession that Jesus was the Son of God – information that Peter knows and that can help propel the story if he is given the chance to reveal it. So he becomes the ideal candidate for the "point of view" role. There is also the unusual nature of Jesus' request regarding the fish and the coin, so it's helpful to see that request through the eyes of a character who might well share our surprise and confusion. Again, it's a case of finding the best way of using a character to bring the audience into the story.

Telling tips: *It might be fun to get everyone to put a finger to a chin and go "Hmmmm?" every time the word "question" appears.*

Questions. It had been a trip full of questions. And Peter's head was tired of trying to find the answers.

"Who do people say Jesus is?"

"Who do I think Jesus is?"

"Why is Jesus standing there with two long-dead prophets?"

"Why can't we heal a poor sick boy like Jesus does?"

Questions, questions and more questions!

So Peter went for a walk through the streets of Capernaum to get away from the questions. And, out of the blue, two tax collectors walked right up to him with – you guessed it – questions.

"Does your teacher pay the temple tax?" the first one demanded to know.

"Ummm..." said Peter, scratching his head.

"It takes a lot of money to run the temple," grunted the second one.

"Yes, well..." Peter nodded.

"Two drachmas a head. That's the charge," insisted the first.

"That much?" Peter grinned. "Heh-heh." But they did not grin back.

"So does he pay it or not?" the second one repeated. "Jesus, your master?"

"Yes. Sure. Why not?" answered Peter, at last, desperate to get rid of the questions, hoping that his answer would make them go away.

And sure enough, it did.

So Peter sighed a relieved sigh and strolled back to the house where Jesus and the rest of the disciples were staying.

And the moment he opened the door, what did Jesus greet him with?

A question.

"Who do earthly kings collect taxes from?" he asked. "From their own sons, or from others?"

Peter sighed again, but it was not a relieved sigh this time. The wheels in his head were spinning furiously. What did this question have to do with anything?

And then the wheels stopped, because he had his answer.

Somehow Jesus knew about those tax collectors. Somehow Jesus seemed to know about everything. Of course he did. He was the Son of God, after all – at least that's the answer Peter had given to a question a few days before.

And if he was God's Son, and if God was the king of the temple, then, no, he didn't have to pay the temple tax, because kings didn't collect taxes from their own sons!

So that's what Peter answered, fully expecting to bring the matter to an end.

Jesus nodded.

"You're right," he said. "The sons of a king shouldn't have to pay the king's taxes. But at the same time, there's no point offending those temple tax collectors unnecessarily."

And then Jesus smiled one of those smiles. The one that Peter had grown used to seeing. The one that signalled he was up to something!

"So instead of emptying our own pockets," Jesus said, "we'll find the money elsewhere."

Peter looked just a little nervous. Somehow he could feel another question coming. In fact, it was something even more unusual.

"Go to the lake, Peter," Jesus said. "Go to the lake and throw out your line. Then look in the mouth of the first fish you catch. You'll find a four-drachma coin there. Take it – and pay both our temple taxes."

Peter knew better than to ask. He just turned around and walked back out the door.

No question.

A Tale of Two Rabbis

As I write this, I am preaching through the book of Acts at the church I pastor (I've got this thing for multiple-year sermon series) and this retelling is based on the latest passage I'll be dealing with. It's a reflection of the foreshadowing that Luke himself employs throughout Acts – giving you a glimpse of a character before you encounter him fully. In fact, there is a bit of that in the story itself, with regard to Gamaliel, and I have just added a wee bit more. And I have also used what we know about Paul, both from his own letters and from Acts, to try to imagine his reaction to this event.

Telling tips: *You could do this one with someone else – one of you reading the older man's part, and the other reading the younger man.*

The young man and the older man walked slowly down the street together.

"So how did the meeting go?" asked the younger man, deliberately, intensely, eyes fixed on the road ahead.

"Well..." hesitated the older man, like he did not want to answer the question.

"Tell me everything," the younger man continued, oblivious to the hint in his companion's voice. "You arrested the followers of the Nazarene. That much I know."

"And they escaped," sighed the older man. "Miraculously, they say."

"They would," sneered the younger man. "It's always some miracle or other with that lot. I suspect they had a contact inside the prison. So...?"

"So they went back into the streets – and kept on preaching."

"I know the gist," nodded the younger man. "You killed Jesus. You're evil. And God brought him back to life to prove he was the Messiah."

"That's about it," the older man nodded back.

"So you arrested them again, I hope," grunted the younger man.

"Well, 'arrest' might be too strong a word," the older man answered. "They're popular. Their reputation is growing. We have to be careful about public opinion."

"You're spineless," grumbled the younger man. "That's what you mean, isn't it?"

"Again, perhaps too strong a word," the older man responded. "We had them escorted by the guards back into our presence. And we told them, in no uncertain terms, that they had to stop telling people that Jesus had risen from the grave and that we were responsible for his death."

"And...?" said the younger man.

"And they refused," the older man sighed. "And preached one of their sermons to US."

The younger man threw his hands in the air and shook his head. "Did no one stop them?" he raged. "Did no one do anything to shut them up?"

"Yes, yes, of course," the older man answered quickly. "There were calls, right there and then, that they be put to death."

"Excellent," grinned the younger man. "Action at last."

"And then," continued the older man, "Rabbi Gamaliel spoke."

"Gamaliel!" said the younger man, stopping and turning to face his companion. "Even more excellent! I trained under him, you know."

"So you have mentioned," said the older man. Many times, he thought.

"So what did he say?" asked the younger man.

"Well..." answered the older man, hesitating once more. "First he said that the followers of Jesus should be escorted out of the room."

"And flogged?" interrupted the younger man.

"Let me finish. First, they left the room. Then he presented us with a little history lesson."

"He would," the younger man smiled. "Precedents. History. Law. They were at the heart of my training."

"So you have mentioned," said the older man again. "He told us about Theudas, who also claimed to be somebody great. He gained a small following, but was then put to death by the Romans."

"I remember," nodded the younger man. "Another so-called 'messenger from God'. Another imposter."

"And then he reminded us of Judas, the Galilean, who objected to the Roman census."

"Ah yes," smiled the younger man. "That didn't end well either. So his point was, surely, that the followers of Jesus would meet a similar end. Defeated. Scattered. Destroyed."

"Well..." hesitated the older man for a third time.

"Spit it out, man!" demanded his companion. "I want to know!"

"Well, it wasn't quite so straightforward as that. His advice, in essence, was that we leave them alone."

"What!" cried the younger man.

"I knew you wouldn't like it. And you probably won't like this, either. Gamaliel said that if we left them alone and what they were doing was not from God, then it would pass, like the others. But if it was from God, then there was nothing we could do to stop this movement anyway."

"If it was from God?" cried the younger man, again – his voice shrill now, shrieking. "To even consider that possibility is blasphemy! These people defy everything we believe – the Law of Moses, the temple! What was Gamaliel thinking?"

"I don't know," said the older man, quietly. And then he smiled a little smile. "Perhaps you should ask him. He was your teacher, after all."

"Enough! Enough!" roared the younger man, storming away. "I must think. I must think." And then he turned and looked back and said, "And someone must have the courage to act. To be God's hand. To make sure that this movement does not succeed – that each and every one of them disappears."

The older man sighed. "Wait!" he called. "Let's talk. Perhaps

Gamaliel is right. Perhaps there is another way. Wait, Saul. Wait. Don't do anything you'll be sorry for later."

Chariot Wheels

When I set out to write this book, I wanted to include some brand new material. So I decided to retell Bible stories that I had never tackled before. This one is way too violent to have included in *The Lion Storyteller Bible* (yes, I know, my grandma would disagree!) but I have always been intrigued by it, so I thought it would fit nicely here.

This is a perfect example of what can happen when you go back to the text and, as I have suggested, read the whole story. In this case, that had to do with moving beyond the narrative description of the life of Deborah (in Judges 4) and on to the Song of Deborah (in Judges 5). There at the end of the poem is the poignant depiction of Sisera's mother, peering through the latticework, waiting for her son to come home. It's a familiar picture, particularly in light of the numbers of wars raging across the globe at the moment. And even though Sisera is the "bad guy" in this piece, no mother ever looks at her son that way: when he is off to war, he is always fighting on the right side, and all she wants is for him to come home. It's that feeling that I have attempted to bring out in the piece, while still telling the story. And as a result, it demanded that I tell the story, at least in part, from one specific character's point of view.

Telling tips: *You could do this with another person – alternating voices between the sections that describe what Sisera's mum is experiencing (a woman's voice would be best here) and the sections that describe Sisera himself.*

The old woman looked out of the window.

What can be keeping him? she wondered as she watched for the rising dust and listened hard to catch the clatter of iron wheels.

And then the wondering spilled out into words.

"Why is his chariot so long in coming?" she whispered. And then comforted herself with the knowledge that her son commanded nine hundred of those chariots.

Her son. Her warrior. Sisera, leader of the army of King Jabin of Hazor.

She peered through the latticework. Nothing.

Nothing. That's how he had described the army he would face that day.

Israelites. Ants. Crushed under his iron wheels for twenty years now. Destined to be crushed again.

So why was she worried? And why did her hand shake so?

Her lady-in-waiting tiptoed quietly from behind and looked out of the window as well.

"I suspect they are still dividing the spoils," she said. "It can take some time to find them."

And if she had known, and if she could have peered, across the miles – the fields and rivers and hills – she would have seen that Sisera was, indeed, in search of something. But it wasn't the spoils of war. No, with his army routed and his soldiers corpses, he was looking for a place to hide.

"A girl or two for each man," said the lady-in-waiting. "That's what they'll find." And she might have been a prophet.

Bloodied and bruised, Sisera stumbled to the tent of Heber, and found Heber's wife, Jael, standing there.

"I'm thirsty. I'm bleeding. I'm cold," he cried.

So she welcomed him into the tent. She covered him with a blanket and gave him milk to drink.

"Beautiful garments," said the lady-in-waiting. "That's what they'll find. Embroidered clothes for us all."

"I'm exhausted," said Sisera to Jael. "Wait by the door. Let me get just a little rest. And if anyone should come by, tell them there is no one here."

Then he curled up under the blanket and soon was fast asleep.

Sisera's mother looked out of the window. She looked again, in vain.

Jael looked, as well, and she found what she needed straightaway.

A tent peg.

A hammer.

And when she struck the blow, the peg went straight through his temple and, for just a second, he opened his eyes. Like he was looking for something.

"Beautiful clothes," said the lady-in-waiting. "Plunder. The spoils of war, my lady. Just you wait and see."

So the old woman waited.

And the old woman watched.

And listened for the clatter of chariot wheels.

What is the Setting?

What is the setting of the story? That's the question you have to ask next. Many stories are utterly dependent on the audience knowing what the setting is. Imagine the Three Little Pigs without their houses, the Troll without his bridge, or Cinderella without a fancy ballroom. And in the case of Bible stories, there are so many that we know by their settings – The Woman at the Well, The Fiery Furnace, The Storm at Sea.

And those settings are varied and interesting and fun! People who have been Christians for a while have those pictures of what I call "generic Bible land", where every setting is made up of a house with a flat roof, a palm tree on either side, and a camel! But there is so much more to biblical settings than that. And your audience needs to know where they are!

Now, there's no need for a lengthy, flowery description. That may have worked, once upon a time, but these days I think it can unnecessarily slow down the pace of the story. It's the problem that drives the story – remember – and a lot of descriptive language can clog up the traffic! So, as with your characters, keep the descriptions simple and clear. Trust me (or if not me, then all the editors I've ever worked with!) – a few well-chosen words can be more accurate and poetic than a paragraph's-worth of bad ones. Better still, you can sometimes even give your audience the chance to "be" the setting. This won't work with every story, obviously, but it can be very effective with some.

When I tell the story about Jesus calming the storm, I ask the audience to rock gently back and forth. They become the waves on the sea. They become the setting. And not only do they hear about Jesus' power to still storms, but they experience it as well!

You can find hooks in settings, as well, that will help you to shape the story. As I read through the story of Joshua and the Battle of Jericho, the thing that jumped out at me was the fact that they had to march around the walls. So the phrase "round and round" became the hook to tie the story together. The walls go "round and round" the city. Joshua's thoughts spin "round and round" in his head. The angel's sword swings "round and round" his head. The soldiers gather "round and round" to hear the plan. And, last of all, the people, at last, march "round and round" until the walls come tumbling down. It's simple, I know! But as I've suggested many times already, it's usually the simplest ideas that are the best. And when they are connected to the setting, they also help, I think, to make the story more real, more concrete.

The Storm on the Lake

This is my favourite setting-based story; here the crowd is invited to join in with the story, not as characters, but as the setting.

Telling tips: *Ask the audience to be waves and rock back and forth. I always stick my arms out a bit, but you can do it as you like. Tell them to keep rocking as long as you are talking – gently at first and then more wildly as the storm strikes. Then, when Jesus stills the storm, tell them to calm down altogether, and to begin rocking gently again at the end.*

It was a perfect day.

The sky was blue. The lake too.

And a gentle breeze whipped the wave tips white and foamy.

Jesus sat at the side of the lake and talked to the people about God.

"God is your Father," he said. "He dresses the flowers in beautiful colours. He makes sure the birds have enough to eat. But you are his sons and his daughters. Don't you think he can clothe and feed you too?

So trust him, and stop worrying your lives away."

When Jesus had finished teaching, he was tired. So he called his closest friends, and together they piled into a boat and set off across the lake for home.

Jesus yawned. He stretched. He laid his head down and, to the rhythm of the waves and the rocking of the boat, he fell asleep. It was the perfect end to a perfect day!

And then, suddenly, the day was not so perfect.

The sky turned black. The lake too.

And a wild wind stirred the waves up tall and stormy.

The boat rocked right. The boat rocked left. The boat rocked up and down. The boat rocked so hard, in fact, that Jesus' friends were sure they would all drown.

But Jesus slept right through it – except for the odd snuffle and snore.

"Jesus!" his friends called at last. "Jesus! Wake up! We're all going to drown!"

So Jesus woke up. Then he sat up. Then he rubbed his eyes and he stood up. It was all anybody else could do to stay on their feet. But Jesus stood up! And then, very calmly, he said to the wind, "Quiet now." And he said to the waves, "Settle down."

And they did!

Then Jesus turned to his friends and said, "You didn't need to be frightened. You didn't have to worry. All you had to do was trust me.

"See, everything is calm."

And so it was. The sky was blue. The lake too. And the little waves splashed happily at the side of the boat.

It was a perfect day again!

The Walls Fall Down

This is the other story that I use in workshops when I want to give an example of using the setting as the basis for finding a way into the story.

Telling tips: *Divide the audience into three groups: one to your left (the people of Jericho), one in the middle (the wall) and one to your right (the Israelites). Ask the group in the middle to stand in a line, side by side, facing the Israelite group – you may need more than one row, depending on the number in this group – or you could just start by making this group a bit smaller than the others. Also choose someone to play an angel and give them something sharp to wave about. I usually use a pen (one that clicks or has a top is best – because you can cover the point if your volunteer looks a bit over-active!). Then tell the story and encourage everyone to play along. I usually just read the lines of the angel out loud and then get the angel volunteer to shout them after me. I do the same with the people of Jericho when they make fun of the Israelites.*

The walls of Jericho went round and round. Round and round the whole city. The walls were tall. The walls were thick. How would God's people ever get in?

Joshua's thoughts went round and round. Round and round inside his head. He was the leader of God's people now that Moses was dead. But how could he lead them into Jericho?

The sword of the Lord swung round and round. Round and round the angel's head. "God will lead you into Jericho," said the angel to Joshua. "He has a secret plan. All you have to do is trust him."

The soldiers of Israel gathered round and round. Round and round their leader, Joshua. He told them the angel's plan. He didn't leave out one bit. The soldiers were amazed!

So the army of Israel marched round and round. Round and round the walls of Jericho. Once round each day. Six days in a row. And the people of Jericho laughed.

"Why are they marching round and round? Round and round the walls of Jericho? Is this a parade? Is it some kind of trick? They'll never beat us this way!"

But still the army marched round and round, round and round on the seventh day – they marched round once, they marched round twice. They marched round Jericho seven times. Then they raised their voices. They blew their trumpets. And the walls came crashing down!

The people of Israel danced round and round. Round and round the ruins of Jericho. "God is our helper!" they sang and they shouted. "He will never let us down!"

The Fourth Vulture

Here's another story from *Angels, Angels All Around* which I have included in this section because the setting is what I chose to find a way into the story. Hagar is in the desert, sent away by Abraham, and the vultures are circling. It's those vultures, high in the sky, one then two then three then four, which chart the progress of the story and move it along. It's a simple device, but it builds the tension until the fourth vulture swoops down in Hagar's direction.

Telling tips: *I have nothing special to suggest because I think that participation could spoil the mood. Just tell it dramatically on your own.*

One vulture.

Hagar saw him out of the corner of her eye as she raised the water pouch to her son's cracked lips.

Empty. The water was all gone.

And the vulture celebrated with a shrill cry and a lazy loop-the-loop.

Two vultures.

Their wings beat slow and heavy, like hot wind against a tent flap.

Hagar heard them as she picked up little Ishmael and laid him in the scraggly shadow of a desert bush. The bread was gone too. And with it any hope for survival. Hagar cradled her son's head and stroked one sunken cheek.

"Quiet now," she said. "Sleep now."

And in no time, the exhausted boy was off. Hagar gave him a dry kiss, eased his head onto a rolled-up blanket, and sat down a short distance away. She could not bear to watch him die, but she could shield him from the sun's hot stare. And she could chase away the vultures.

Three vultures.

Hagar cursed them, shaking her fist at the sky. But they took no notice. They just chased each other, tracing circles round the face of the sun.

Hagar cursed the sun, too. And the desert – this dry and empty place she was forced to wander.

And then she cursed the day that had brought her here – that day so long ago when everything seemed simple.

She had been a servant girl. And Sarah was her mistress. Sarah, the wife of Abraham – leader of the tribe. Abraham, who left the comforts of city life to find a new land, a land that God had promised to show him.

God had made another promise, too, so they said. Abraham and Sarah would have a son who would be the first child of a mighty new nation. But Abraham and Sarah weren't getting any younger. Indeed, Sarah was already well past her childbearing years.

And that's where Hagar came in.

"Go to my husband," Sarah had ordered her, "and bear his child. I am too old. God's promise is surely not for me. But perhaps through you, Abraham will see the promise come true."

Hagar had obeyed her mistress. She had given birth to Ishmael. And, for a time, everyone had been happy. Then, several years later, Sarah miraculously became pregnant too, and gave birth to a son she called Isaac. From that moment, Hagar's happiness had begun to flicker and fade, till it finally disappeared like some desert mirage.

Sarah's jealousy was the problem. She feared that Ishmael and not Isaac would receive Abraham's inheritance, because he had been born first. So she made life miserable for Hagar and Ishmael, and finally persuaded Abraham to send them away into the desert.

So now, along with the desert and the vultures and the sun, Hagar cursed Sarah, her jealous mistress. She nearly cursed Abraham too. Abraham, her master and the father of her son. But then she remembered that look in his eyes as he sent them away.

The look that said, "I don't want to do this."

The look that said, "I can't find any other way."

The look that said, "I believe things will be all right."

Were those looks real, Hagar wondered. Or were they just mirages? Were those tears in the old man's eyes, or just a reflection of the desert sun?

Four vultures.

And the fourth bigger than the rest.

What did it matter anyway? thought Hagar. In a short time, both she and Ishmael would be dead. The vultures would get their dinner. Sarah would get her way. And Abraham would still get what his God had promised – a son, a family, a mighty nation.

Abraham's God had been good to him. Oh, that he would be so good to her.

And yet there had been a time, Hagar remembered, a time when God had been good to her. A time shortly before her son had been born, when Sarah's jealousy was just beginning to brew. A time when she had fled, afraid of Sarah's evil temper.

Then God had sent an angel to comfort her. "Call your son Ishmael," the angel had told her. "The name means 'God has heard.'"

Ishmael was moaning. She could hear him crying out in his sleep. Would his name hold true? Hagar wondered. Would God hear him now?

One vulture.

At the sound of the boy's cry, the fourth vulture cried back – long and hard and fierce. And instead of descending on their victim, the other three vultures flew away.

Hagar ran to Ishmael, ran to the bush, ran to rescue him from the great dark bird that still remained. She threw herself over her son, wrapped herself around him, buried her head, shut her eyes and waited.

The fourth vulture dropped lower, in ever shrinking circles. It grew larger and larger the closer it got, until it was a huge winged shadow, blocking out the scorching eye of the sun. It hovered over Hagar and Ishmael, hanging low in the air. And then the vulture spoke!

"Don't be afraid," it said. "God has heard the cries of your son. See, I have chased away the vultures. I have shielded you from the sun. And now I have something to show you."

Slowly, Hagar lifted her head and looked up.

Round, dark eyes.

Black, feathery hair.

And a sharp beak of a nose.

The face that greeted her looked much like a bird's. But the kindness and love in that face could only have come from somewhere far beyond the sky. And she knew in a moment that the wings beating above her were angel's wings.

Like a mother cradling twin children, the angel lifted Hagar and Ishmael into its wings, and then onto its back. They flew straight for the sun, high above the desert, until they could see for miles in every direction.

The angel turned to the north. "There is Abraham's camp, the place from which you came."

Then it turned to the south. "There is an oasis – with food and water, where you can rest and live!"

Finally, it turned to the east. "And there – do you see it? All that land and the land beyond? That is the land that will one day belong to your son Ishmael and to his sons after him."

And then the angel dived straight for the oasis. And the swiftness of the dive startled Hagar, sent her hair whipping round her head, and made her clutch tightly the soft feathers that surrounded her. But even the speed of the descent could not shake the smile that now rested on Hagar's face.

When they reached the shimmering pool, Hagar filled her water pouch until it wanted to burst. The she poured the water into Ishmael's mouth and over his face, and into her mouth too. And when she had drunk her fill, she turned to thank the angel.

But it was gone. The sky was empty. The sun had begun to set – no longer the burning eye of an enemy, but the warm, watchful gaze of a friend.

And that's when Hagar gave thanks to God.

For one angel.

One promise.

And no more vultures.

What is the Problem?

Every story has one central problem. And it is the problem that drives the story – that makes the listener stay with the story to the end to discover how that problem is resolved. Will Cinderella get to the ball? Will Red Riding Hood escape the wolf? Will the tortoise win the race, or will the hare? Those are the problems that push these stories along. So the problem needs to be stated early and then used to build the tension throughout the story.

The difficulty is that, unlike finding the characters or the setting, finding the main problem is sometimes a little more tricky.

With some stories, there is more than one central problem to choose from. Is the story of Zacchaeus about a bad man who needs forgiveness, a lonely man who needs acceptance, a short man who can't see, or a town that needs to understand Jesus' priorities regarding the company he keeps? The main problem could be any of these, but it can't really be all of them – not in one story, anyway. You have to choose which problem *you* want to drive the story, right from the start, because the way you tell the story (the point of view you choose, the participation exercises you use – everything in fact) will depend upon the problem you want to resolve.

You could say the same thing about the problem in the prodigal son. The problem could be, "Will my dad take me back?" The problem could be "Will my son come back?" The problem could be "Why did my dad take my brother back?" There is a sense in which the problem you choose depends partly on your own preference, and partly on the needs of the group for whom you are preparing the story. But you still have to choose.

There's another potential difficulty. It's not uncommon for stories to have too many problems to solve in one sitting. The story of Joseph, extremely familiar now because of *Joseph and the Amazing Technicolor Dreamcoat*, is a good example of that. The story comes to us in several episodes: Joseph the dreamer, Joseph the slave, Joseph the servant of Potiphar, Joseph the prisoner, Joseph the ruler, and Joseph the saviour of his people. Each of those episodes has its own driving problem. So it might be best to tell it in several sittings, or at least as several episodes.

Finally, the problem you choose to drive a story might have something to do with the age and maturity of your audience.

The story of Jonah is a good case in point. When children are very small, we sometimes just tell them about a man who was swallowed by a big fish (or a whale). As they get older we tend to focus on Jonah's disobedience as the main problem. But a closer inspection (particularly of that bit at the end) reveals that the problem in "Jonah" is actually all about racism. That's right – racism! Jonah's disobedience is due to the fact that he hates the people of Nineveh and does not want God to save them. That's why he sits on the hill, at the end, and watches over the city. He's waiting – waiting for them to fall back into their evil ways, in the hope that God will destroy them after all. So what does God do? He grows a tree to give Jonah shade. And then he sends a worm to kill the tree. And when Jonah complains that the tree is dead, God brings him face to face with his upside-down priorities. "You care about this tree," God sighs, "but you care nothing for a city full of people who do not know their right hand from their left." And that's where the story ends! We never even get to hear Jonah's response. Why? Because the original storyteller – the person who wrote the book of Jonah – wanted the reader, wanted the hearer, to provide his or her own response. Will we love those whom God loves (even though they are different, even though they are our enemies)? Or will we continue in our prejudice and hate?

It's a powerful story, Jonah. But it's even more powerful (and surely more appropriate to our day and age) when you understand the true nature of its problem.

So, choose your problem – that's the key thing – for it will affect everything else you do.

The Runaway's Tale

Let's start with Jonah, a Bible story in which choosing the "problem" is slightly different; it's an example of the way that the "problem" changes, sometimes, depending on the maturity of the hearers. I have included the introduction to this retelling, originally from *More Bible Baddies*, because I think it helps to make my point even clearer.

Telling tips: *As with the other longer pieces, it's best to just tell it dramatically.*

There's nothing cute about the story of Jonah. I know that people think there is – that the big fish makes it the perfect story for little kids. But that's only because they don't understand what the story is about.

You see, this story is not about disobedience, even though Jonah did disobey God when he ran away from the mission God had set for him. And it's not about deliverance, either, even though Jonah is rescued from the fish and the city of Nineveh escapes destruction as a result of his message. No, the story of Jonah is all about prejudice. That's right – good old-fashioned bigotry and hate. And as far as I can tell, there's nothing cute about that.

Jonah admits as much. The people of Nineveh are not like him. They worship different gods. They are "the enemy". And he refuses to go and speak to them, not because he is afraid of what they will do to him, but because he is afraid of what God will do for them, if they respond to his message.

And that is why the story of Jonah ends so abruptly – not with an answer, but with a question. Because the author's concern is not whether Jonah laid aside his prejudices and decided to love whomever God loves. His concern is with what his readers will do. And the answer, therefore, is up to you and me.

It didn't make any sense.

The words came to him, in an instant, unexpected, like they always had. The voice was the same, unmistakable – God himself, the Maker of heaven and earth. But the message made no sense. No sense at all.

"Go to Nineveh, the great city, and speak my words against it. For I have seen its wickedness."

The first part – the part about wickedness – Jonah understood. For Nineveh was the capital of Assyria. And Assyria was Israel's greatest enemy – not only because of her powerful army, which might sweep down at any time and destroy his people, but also because of her great immorality. Idol worshippers. Pig eaters. That's what the Assyrians were. Everything they did and everything they believed was directly opposed to the holy Law that God had given Israel – the Law that Jonah had been taught to cherish and obey. They were enemies, and pagans, intent on destroying God's chosen people, the Hebrews, and yet, God had told Jonah to go and speak to them.

And that is what Jonah did not understand. That is what made no sense. For Jonah knew his prophet's job well: Speak God's word. Deliver God's message. And hope that those who received the message would listen, and repent, and be granted God's mercy and blessing.

God's blessing on Nineveh? God's mercy – showered on the enemy of God's people? Even the possibility was unthinkable. And that is why Jonah ran away.

It didn't make any sense. Not really. Jonah couldn't run away from God, and he knew it. But he didn't want any part of the mission that God had set for him, either. So he decided that the simplest solution would be for him to get as far away from Nineveh as possible. Nineveh was east, and therefore Jonah headed west.

He went to Joppa, first – on the coast. And there he booked passage on a ship set for Tarshish, at the western end of the Great Sea. And all went well, until a storm came thundering out of nowhere.

"This doesn't make any sense!" the captain thought. Every sailor sat on his knees, praying. But the passenger was down in the hold, asleep, as if nothing in the world was wrong.

"Wake up!" the captain shouted, shaking Jonah till he stirred. "What's the matter with you? The ship is about to break in two and you are down here sleeping. Get up! Pray to your god! And maybe he will save us."

Jonah prayed. Or, at least, he bowed his head. But the storm did not subside. Not even a little. So the sailors drew straws, determined to find out who was responsible for their troubles. And the short straw went to Jonah.

"Who are you? Where do you come from?" they demanded to know. "And what have you done that could have brought such evil upon us?"

Jonah looked at the sailors and sighed. There wasn't an Israelite among them. They were pagans, one and all. Pig eaters. Idol worshippers. How could they possibly understand?

"I am a Hebrew," he explained. "And I worship the Lord God, the God who made the earth and sea – and everything else that is! He is the One I am running from. He is the One who is responsible for this storm."

The sailors trembled. "What can we do, then? Tell us – how do we appease your God? How do we stop the storm?"

"There is only one way," said Jonah slowly, "You must throw me into the sea."

It didn't make any sense. The sailors should have jumped at Jonah's offer. They should have chucked him overboard and gone safely on their way. But they didn't. Instead, they took up their oars and rowed even harder for shore, hoping to outrun the storm.

"Was it possible?" Jonah wondered. "Were these pig eaters, these idol worshippers, actually trying to save him?"

Whatever the intention, their efforts proved futile. For the harder they rowed, the higher rose the sea around them. Until, at last, they were left without a choice. Either Jonah would drown, or they all would.

So they fell to their knees again – and Jonah could hardly believe this – they prayed not to their own gods, but to the Lord!

"God, God of heaven and earth!" they cried. "Forgive us for what we are about to do."

Then they tossed Jonah overboard, and immediately the sea grew calm. And as the prophet sank deeper and deeper beneath the waves, they worshipped the prophet's God and offered sacrifices to his name.

It didn't make any sense. Somehow, Jonah was still alive! He could hear himself breathing. He could feel his heart beating. And the smell

– phew! – he had never smelled anything so awful in his life! But when he opened his eyes, everything was dark.

He shook his head and tried to remember. He remembered the crashing waves. He remembered struggling for the surface and saving each tiny bit of breath. And then, just before he passed out... he remembered! The fish! The biggest fish he had ever seen! And it was swimming straight for him.

Was it possible? Jonah wondered. It must be. It had to be! He was sitting in the belly of the fish!

And, no, it still didn't make any sense. Jonah had disobeyed God. He knew he deserved to die. And yet, God had preserved him, sent this fish – he was sure of it! And that meant, surely it meant, that God still had work for him to do, and that he would see the light of day again!

And so Jonah prayed a prayer. Not a prayer for help, but a prayer of thanksgiving, as if the help had already come. As if the belly of this fish were a temple, and he was seated in the midst of it – ribs standing tall like pillars, the odour of entrails rising like incense.

"I cried to God," prayed Jonah,
"I cried to him and he answered me.
From the belly of hell I cried
And the Lord God heard my voice!

"It was he who cast me in the sea,
Far beneath the crashing waves,
With the waters roaring round me,
And the surface like the sky.

"And so I thought
that I had been banished,
Cut off from God
And his temple forever.

"Down I went,
Down deeper and deeper,

Down to the feet of the mountains,
Seaweed wrapped around my head.

"Down, still further down,
Down, and no escape.
And that is when you touched me
And rescued me from the watery pit.

"In the nick of time,
Just when all hope had gone,
You heard my prayer, O Lord,
Far, far away, in your holy temple.

"Idol worshippers don't understand.
Their petitions count for nothing.
But I will give you thanks,
Offer sacrifices in your name,
For you are my great deliverer!"

Three days and three nights. That's how long Jonah waited in the belly of the fish. Then it belched him up on dry land, and those words came pouring into his head again:

"Go to Nineveh, the great city, and tell them that I have seen their wickedness."

It still didn't make any sense. Not to Jonah. But he wasn't about to argue this time. So he travelled east, all the way to Nineveh. And when he got there, his mission made less sense than ever!

"This city it enormous!" sighed Jonah. "It will take me days just to walk across it. How can my message possibly make any difference?"

But Jonah was determined not to end up in another fish's belly. So he started to preach.

"Forty days!" he said to anyone who would listen. "Forty days to change your ways. Or else God is going to destroy your city."

"This is useless!" Jonah sighed. "These pig eaters, these idol worshippers, are never going to change."

But day after day, he preached. And day by day, the people of Nineveh began to take notice. There were just a few, at first, but soon the whole city was on its knees – from the humblest servant to the king himself – weeping and praying and asking God's forgiveness.

"This doesn't make any sense!" Jonah grumbled.

"No sense at all!" Jonah groused.

"You had the perfect opportunity, God, to destroy your enemy, and the enemy of your people. But you let it pass, and now – look at them – pig eaters and idol worshippers, praying, confessing, repenting, and asking for forgiveness!

"Can you see, now, why I ran away? This won't last. They'll be up to their old tricks again, in no time – you'll see! And then they'll be out to destroy us all over again."

And at that moment, Jonah got an idea.

"I'll get out of the city," he said to himself, "I'll get out of the city and sit on the hillside and watch. Watch and wait for them to turn from God again. And maybe then God will destroy the Ninevites once and for all!"

"Jonah," God called.

"Jonah!" God beckoned. "Do you really think it's right for you to be angry with me?"

But Jonah paid God no attention. He was too busy building a little tent and stocking it with provisions, ready to watch the city's ruin.

So God got Jonah's attention another way. He made a tree grow up over Jonah's tent, to shade him in the heat of the day. And just as Jonah had started to appreciate the shade, God sent a worm in the night to kill the little tree.

"This doesn't make any sense!" Jonah moaned. "This tree was here one day, and gone the next. Now I'll have to sit and sweat. Life is so unfair!"

And that's when the voice, the unmistakable voice, the voice of God himself, came pouring, once again, into Jonah's head.

"I'll tell you what makes no sense, Jonah," the voice began. "You grieve at the death of this tree, but you have no concern, whatsoever, for the lives – the thousands of lives – who dwell in the city below.

"Yes, they are idol worshippers, so far from understanding me as a child is from knowing its right or left hand. But I love them. And I have forgiven them. And if my ways are ever going to make any sense to you, then you will have to lay aside your prejudices and learn to love them too."

If

Sometimes it helps an audience to understand a story if you draw a great big imaginary arrow and point it at one aspect of the story. That's what I've done here. The devil wants to call into question Jesus' messiahship and the way he intends to bring that about. So, as he did in the Garden of Eden, he tries to cast doubt into Jesus' mind. And he does so by raising a series of "ifs". The word, in fact, lies at the heart of the problem of the story – it's the way "in" to understand it. And that's why I have included it here.

Telling tips: *You could use two or three people to retell this, depending on whether or not you provide one of the voices: one to narrate, one to be Jesus and one to be the devil.*

Forty days in the desert.
Forty days without food.
Forty days and then the devil comes.
And the word he comes with is "if".
(The conjunction, the question, the conditional clause, the doubt.)

"If you are the Son of God," he says. "You can speak to these stones and turn them into bread."

So Jesus speaks. Not to the stones, but to the devil. And there are no "ifs". Or "ands", for that matter. And only one "but".

"Man does not live on bread alone," he says, "but (there it is!) on every word that comes from the mouth of God."

Forty days in the desert.

Forty days without food.

Forty days and now he's standing on the topmost part of the temple.

And again the word the devil has for him is "if".

(The conjunction, the question, the conditional clause, the doubt.)

"If you are the Son of God," he says. "Jump. For according to the word of God (and here he smiles and winks), the angels will come to your rescue."

Jesus winks back and gives his answer. No "ifs". No "ands". And this time, no "buts" either.

"Don't put the Lord your God to the test," he grins. "His word says that, as well."

Forty days in the desert.

Forty days without food.

And now he's on a mountain top, the kingdoms of the world spread out before him.

And from the devil, yet one more "if".

(The conjunction, the question, the conditional clause, the doubt.)

"If you bow down and worship me," he says. "All of this will be yours."

So Jesus answers. No "ifs". No "ands". No "buts".

"Go away!" he says. "For it is written: worship God and serve him only."

So the devil goes. And all his "ifs" with him.

(The conjunctions, the questions, the conditional clauses, the doubts.)

And the angels come and care for the Son of God.

No "ifs".

No "ands".

No "buts".

Moving

Again, this story reduces the problem to one word, and then uses a repetitive device with that word to move the story along and to tie it together.

Telling tips: *You could ask the group to say the word "moving" and make a simple moving motion – turning to one side, maybe.*

Moving.

Jesus was moving – moving through the city of Jerusalem – when he came upon a pool by the Sheep Gate. A pool called Bethesda.

Moving.

No one was moving there. For the pool was surrounded by the blind, who couldn't see to move. By the lame, who couldn't get up to move. And by the paralysed, who couldn't move at all.

Moving.

But the water in the pool was moving. Moving every now and then. Rumour had it that an angel of the Lord moved the water, stirring it, from time to time, with his heavenly hand. And the first one in the water would be healed.

Moving.

That was the key thing. Moving into the water first.
So the blind would have helpers to lead them there.
The lame would have helpers to lift them to their feet.
And the paralysed would have helpers to carry them.

Moving.

Jesus watched it all. But he found one man's plight particularly moving.

"I've been an invalid for thirty-eight years," explained the man. "But I have no one to help me into the water. So someone else always gets there before me."

Moving.

"Do you want to start moving?" Jesus asked.

"Of course!" replied the man.

"Then pick up your mat and walk," said Jesus.

And he did! Just like that.

Moving.

And while the others moved towards the water, the man simply picked up his mat and walked away.

Moving.

Stop and Go

Again, the problem of the story is reduced in this retelling to a couple of simple words. I think this approach always makes pieces more accessible and more memorable.

Telling tips: *Divide your group into four parts. The first three groups just say "Go!" when you point to them. So "Go!" (first group), "Go!" (second) and "Go!" (third). You might even want to have them stretch out their arms and point when they do so. Then the final group shouts "Stop!" when you point to them and hold out one hand in a stopping motion like a traffic cop.*

Go! Go! Go!

It was all go.

Antioch. Derbe. Lystra. And a positive response to the good news about Jesus, wherever Paul went.

He had a young, enthusiastic new helper called Timothy. Ahead lay the whole of Asia. It was time to go.

But then the Holy Spirit spoke to Paul. And he had a different idea.

Stop!

That's what the Spirit said. Asia may be nice. Rugged scenery. Lovely people. But I have something else in mind for you.

So Paul and his companions wandered along the edge of Asia and came finally to the borders of Bithynia.

Go! Go! Go!

That's what Paul thought – across the border and into a place where no one had heard about Jesus.

But, once again, the Holy Spirit had a different idea.

Stop!

That's what the Spirit said. Bithynia is beautiful. And the beaches? Well... you could write a book. But I have something else in mind for you.

So Paul turned away from Bithynia. He passed by Mysia, as well. And finally came to the coast at Troas, where he stopped. He had no choice, for he had no idea where to go.

And then, in the night, Paul had a vision. A vision of a man from Greece.

"Come and help us!" That's all the man said. And that was all the information Paul needed.

And when the morning came, he and his companions didn't stop for anything. They boarded a ship and set sail for Greece.

For it was time, at last, to go.

To Go! Go! Go!

Find the Tension

Having spent the time to look at the characters, the setting, and the problem of the story you want to retell, you should not only have found some element in the story that makes it "shine" for you, you should also have some idea of how to retell it. In Chapter 4, I talk about the kind of storytelling "tricks of the trade" that will help you to do that, but there is just one more aspect of the structure of the story that you will need to consider and that is the pacing of the story – how you find your way from beginning to middle to end.

I read an article, several years ago, written by a man who doctors screenplays. Sadly, I can't remember who wrote the article or even where I found it, but what it said has stuck with me ever since.

The author suggested that you should divide your story into three parts – but not three equal parts. In the case of an average two-hour film, he suggested that the first part should be thirty minutes, the final part thirty minutes, with an hour-long section in between. Obviously, you are unlikely to be telling two-hour stories, but the proportions should remain the same.

In the first thirty minutes, he suggested, a good writer gets his character "up a tree". In other words, he introduces the main characters and establishes the problem.

It's the problem that's driving the story, remember? And unless the audience knows what the problem is, and understands it clearly – then you're just coasting! So this makes a huge amount of sense.

In the next section – that hour-long one in the middle – he said that he throws stones at the character in the tree. In other words, he gives the characters problems to overcome along the way to solving the main problem. This is what builds tension towards the resolution, and leads the listener to the place where they desperately want to know how it all ends – how the problem is solved.

Traditional stories often make use of the "group of three" rule, here. The troll meets not one, not two, but *three* Billy Goats Gruff before he is defeated. The Big Bad Wolf blows down two houses and tries his best to knock down a third before he ends up down the chimney. And even Jesus used groups of three. In the parable of the Good Samaritan, the man who was beaten isn't saved until passer-by number three comes on the scene.

I'm not suggesting that you artificially create three events in the middle of a story if that's not appropriate to retelling that particular tale. It's the proportions that are important to remember. If there is too much going on (the Big Bad Wolf moves from the house of straw, to the house of sticks, to the house of bricks, to the house of concrete blocks, and so on!) your audience will get bored. But by the same token, if there is too little going on (the Big Bad Wolf blows down the first house and eats all the pigs) then there is no tension at all – and no story, really either. Just an unfortunate incident! To borrow a phrase from Goldilocks, a little girl who also had to deal with a group of three, the middle has to be "just right!"

And finally, there is The End! That's the place where, according to the article I read, you get your character out of the tree – you solve the problem. Quite simply, it has to be punchy and precise. If there is some phrase that you have repeated throughout, you might want to finish with it. Or perhaps with some action you have asked your audience to do. What you want to avoid is just trailing off, like the "fade" at the end of a pop song. Resolve your problem – make a big deal of it – and then tie it up nice and neatly.

There is nothing more satisfying than a good ending. So I will often try to decide, quite early on in my preparation of a story, how I will go about finishing it. And there's nothing more wonderful than the "ooh" or the "aww" or the "wow" or just the stunned silence you get from an audience when an ending has worked well.

Chapter Four
Storytelling Tips and Techniques

The Place of Play

When I was a boy, I had lots of little plastic dinosaurs and farm animals and toy soldiers and cars and trucks. On the days that we couldn't go outside, my two brothers and I would take all of those little plastic toys, dump them into a pile on the middle of the floor, and spend ages choosing which ones we wanted on our "team". Then, when all the choosing was done, we'd act out little adventures with those toys. We'd visit each other's "houses", and drive around in the cars, and at some point a battle would inevitably break out, and somebody's toys would go flying down the stairs!

What were we doing? We were playing. And when it comes down to it, I believe that's what storytelling is all about. It's play – a verbal kind of play. So whenever I prepare to stand before a crowd, the first thing I do is to go to the "place of play". I'm not sure where that is, exactly. It's in my head, and in my memories, and in my heart, all at once. But I know when I'm there. And I think that the children I share the stories with know that too. It's like they can see it in my eyes, sense it in my voice, pick up on it as we build that all-important relationship. It's a place they're familiar with, you see. And a place where adults seldom go. So when they see an adult in the place of play, it makes a difference – it really does. They lean forward, they listen, and they smile. And they want to see what is going to happen next!

Good storytelling begins with being in the place of play. Why? Because kids love it when adults go there. If you're a parent or a grandparent or a teacher, you know exactly what I mean. When you take the time to get down on your hands and knees and join your children in play, they are surprised and delighted all at once. And I think that's because, for just a short while, we crawl into their world – with their rules and expectations –instead of forcing them into our world. Frankly, I think the same thing applies to storytelling with adults. One of the reasons they enjoy it is because they get to "play", to be children again, for a while, to go to some never-never land, some once-upon-a-time place, and be in touch with the best kinds of childhood memories. I know that's true, not only because of what I see in the expressions of the adults who enjoy a good story, but also because of what I have seen in the eyes of those who try their hardest to resist it. I've told lots of stories in all-age family services over the years, and there are always a few adults in every church who really struggle with that experience. For some reason – maybe because their own childhood wasn't a happy time – they just don't want to go to that place of play. And they know that's where a story will take them.

Being in the place of play simply makes it easier to be a good storyteller. When I'm in the place of play, I'm relaxed, I'm looking forward to what will happen next, it's easier to respond to the unexpected, and I'm in the mood to have fun (which is even possible with quite serious stories). When I'm not in the place of play – when I'm tired, maybe, or just not happy to be in front of a crowd on that day – I can feel the difference, I really can. I'm tense, I'm more nervous, I'm less likely to pick up on those little things that happen in the audience and help to make the stories come alive. It's simply harder to build that all-important relationship. I don't see or hear the audience as clearly as usual. I get frustrated more easily if things go wrong. It's a bit like sports, I guess. When a football player or a tennis player is relaxed and into the game, then there's a flow, an energy to what they do that can turn even the biggest mistake into something good. For a storyteller – that "zone" is the place of play.

The place of play is also a place of commitment. When children play, they rarely do it half-heartedly. They throw themselves into it – doing whatever the game, the scenario or situation demands. When I was a kid, I can't ever remember saying to my friends, "Sorry, it's a bit embarrassing to have to pretend I'm a monster today." Yes, we'd argue about who had to play what role, but that was always because there were some roles that were just plain better – usually because they were more, rather than less, outrageous. Children can tell if you're in the place of play by your willingness to "go for it" – to set aside the normal adult inhibitions and act in the joyful, unrestrained way that they do. And when you're in the place of play, you're more likely to want to go there, yourself.

"But what about the other adults in the room?" people often ask me. "I'm all right when I'm on my own with the kids," they say, "but I don't want to look a fool in front of my friends or workmates or the other people in my church." All I can suggest is this. Your willingness to go to the place of play and look like a fool will not only bring joy to the children in your audience (and get them on "your side"), it will bring a little joy into the lives of your friends and colleagues, as well! And what could be wrong with that? And I don't just mean that in a "laugh *at* you and not *with* you" kind of way. The silliness, the goofiness, the joyful surprises or the honest tears that are a part of the best kind of storytelling – those simple and basic emotions – are the very ones that get suffocated as we become older and more sophisticated. Storytelling can set them free, and set a part of us free along with them.

There are some groups, however, who are not that keen on going to the place of play, and they make the hardest audiences. Adolescents, particularly, can be difficult (although I have even experienced this among younger children), especially in settings where groups from one or more schools have come together. There's a fear about not appearing "cool" in front of their peers, which often makes them very quiet and unresponsive. These groups require a slightly different approach.

It starts with remembering that "relationship" thing again. Your goal is not to embarrass your audience (well, not until you know them, anyway!), so you do the best you can do and start with a story that's pitched where you think they are. If they're sitting back, arms folded, with that "too-cool-for-storytelling" look in their eyes, don't start with something that's too young, too silly, or requires too much participation. Give them something you're confident with, so that you can watch their reactions and find out what they like. Test the waters with a little participation. Will anyone volunteer? How do the others react? Try several different kinds of humour, as well. Do they laugh the hardest at slapstick, wordplay, or sarcasm? Find out what works and go with that. If, for some reason, you're committed to a serious story, then be real with it – give it everything you've got. I've discovered that teenagers, in particular, can really get into a serious story, partly I think because it shows that you're taking them seriously. You're not treating them like children, but like the adults they consider themselves to be. Whatever you do – keep watching them. Get your energy from those who are responding positively. Ignore, for a while at least, those who insist on training their eyes on the ceiling. They will come along as more of the others do. You can count on it. And by the end of the session (this is my experience, anyway), they'll be "playing" along with the rest of the audience – although they'd be horrified if you were to call it that!

Bringing Characters to Life

One of my all-time favourite stories is "Aunt Mabel's Table". It's one of the first ones I ever wrote and I've told it hundreds and hundreds of times. So many times, in fact, that when the marketing and sales people at my publisher accompany me to promotional events, they run screaming from the room at the first words of the introduction! Every storyteller has a few stories like "Aunt Mabel's Table" – stories that work so well, and they enjoy telling so much, that they can hardly keep themselves from doing it!

"Aunt Mabel" works for a couple of reasons, I think. It has an interesting problem (that's what drives the story – remember?). Five dinner guests. Five cans of food. You have to eat whatever is in the can you choose. But none of the cans has a label. It's like a culinary version of Russian roulette!

But what really makes the story work is the variety of characters around the table. There is Aunt Mabel, for a start, who has invented this little "game". At one point in the story, she is described as being "a little different from other people". There is her husband, Uncle Joe, who has allergic reactions to just about everything. There are her children, Sue (who is probably the most normal of the lot), and Tom, who got dog food the last time they played the game! And then there is Alexander – the visiting nephew – from whose point of view the story is told. These characters are talking constantly – guessing what is in each can and commenting on the contents. And so it's important that the audience can easily distinguish one from the other. That's the challenge of bringing a character to life.

When I first told this story, I took a hard at look at each of the characters and, as I suggested in the previous chapter, I found a couple of adjectives to describe each one. Then I tried to find a voice, a set of expressions, and a posture to "portray" each character.

Aunt Mabel stands up straight and tall, her hands folded in front of her. Her voice is high and posh, with just a hint of barely disguised eccentricity! She smiles almost all the time – because she loves her strange little game.

Uncle Joe, on the other hand, hates the game. He's stooped over. He's grumpy. And he's loud! "That sounds like the lumpy meat spread you always buy!" he shouts. "The kind that makes me burp!"

Cousin Sue doesn't like the game either. But she knows it's not going away, so her voice suggests a sense of sad resignation.

Cousin Tom is a bit of a geek. He's got a nasal voice and a buck-toothed expression that I use to convey his hope that he won't end up with yet another can of dog food.

And Alexander? He's confused and nervous and just a little frightened by this curious dining experience. So I make his voice and actions small and tentative.

Aunt Mabel is obviously not a Bible story, but the same principles apply. A good example is my retelling of the story of Daniel in the Lions' Den. This first appeared in *Angels, Angels All Around*, and then it was turned into a stand-alone picture book, *Dinner in the Lions' Den*, complete with some amazing illustrations by Tim Raglin.

I usually tell the story on my own, so once again it's key that the audience knows the difference between the characters. Daniel was quite old when he was chucked into the lions' den, so I walk with a stoop and give him a croaky old-timer's voice. Father Lion gets a deep, growly voice, Mother Lion a high-pitched ladylike voice. The cubs sound like the little kids they are. And the angel is boomy and Brian Blessed-like. With the lions, I adopt a crouching kind of posture, while the angel stands tall – again simply to suggest a difference and to make sure the audience knows who is speaking.

The idea is to make the characters interesting, funny and distinct, and to do it as simply as possible, so that the change from one character to another doesn't interrupt the smooth flow of the story. That's why I have a problem with using lots of props and costumes. If I'm telling the story on my own, then the time that it takes to change hats or wigs or shirts or whatever usually distracts the audience from the story itself. The trick is to keep it simple – to find just the right "face" or just the right "posture" so that the character can be recognized immediately. Try them out in front of a mirror. That's one of the easiest ways to see if your expressions or postures work. If they make you laugh, then they will probably make your audience laugh, as well. When my brother Tim was a kid, he used to spend hours in the bathroom. We thought he had digestive problems, but it turns out that he was just practising his silly faces! I'm sure that's one of the reasons he's so good at doing them now. And you will find better faces, too, if you try them out and work at them (and are part of a family with really strong bladders!). So think about your characters, try out a few faces and postures, and keep the characterization clear but simple.

And that brings us to character voices. Lots of aspiring storytellers have told me that they struggle creating voices, but I'm convinced that most people can do voices – five, at the very least! Let's take a look at each one:

1. The "high and squeaky" voice is one that most people can do – a voice that would suit a little child, or a fairy, or a baby bird type character. I find that this voice works particularly well if you're a big guy. Kids love the humour that comes from that kind of contrast. So have a go. Why not try it out, right now! Take the first couple of lines of "Twinkle, twinkle little star" and say them in the highest and squeakiest and funniest voice you can do. If you do, you'll notice that that little voice is echoing around somewhere at the top of your throat, right smack in the middle.

2. The "high, scratchy" voice is made by just moving the "high and squeaky" voice to the back of your throat. This voice is great for squirrels and rabbits and hedgehogs and the like. It's cheekier than the

pure high voice and works well with really mischievous characters. So go on. Try the "Twinkle, twinkle" thing again with that voice. It's at the top and the back of your throat.

3. The "big, deep and boomy" voice comes from right at the bottom of your throat, but back in that echoey middle part again. It's great for kings and giants. That's right – go on and try it. "Twinkle, twinkle" would be all right again – but you might want to use "Fee-fi-fo-fum" this time to get just the right idea!

4. The "rough, growly" voice comes from deep in the back of your throat again. This one works for angry giants or lions or tigers or anything really that's meant to be big and scary. A little warning, though – this one will make you want to clear your throat afterwards, and even cough sometimes – and so might interrupt the flow of the story. Someone also told me once that this voice is not particularly good for your throat and could cause damage if used too much. So use it sparingly. That will make it even more effective! So go on and try it, just to see how it works for you.

5. The "nasal" voice is initially created by pinching your nose, just below the bridge, and speaking. This voice is great for those geeky characters. Practise this for a while and you'll find that it won't be long before you can do it without the "pinching" bit.

So you see, there are five voices that anyone can do. And when you add your own voice – there are six! The fact of the matter is that you probably won't need any more than that in the average story. But if you want to add some variation from story to story, you can always play around with whatever regional accents you can do. The UK is blessed with a wonderful variety of regional accents that can make for some very interesting characters and really bring stories to life.

I would encourage you to use accents as well, with a couple of warnings. First, you need to feel pretty confident about your accent before you use it. There's nothing better than when the audience recognizes and laughs along with a really good accent. And nothing worse than when the audience gives you that puzzled look that shows they can't figure out what it is you're trying to do! So it's probably best not to "try out" an accent in the place from which that accent comes! Developing your Geordie accent in Swansea might go down just fine. But don't work on your Welsh one there!

It might also be sensible to avoid purely ethnic accents. There's a fine line here, I know. And it changes from culture to culture. But as a white Westerner, I would feel uncomfortable doing an Asian, Middle Eastern, or "black" voice. It's too easy to stereotype. And, yes, I know that you could say the same thing about regional accents – but there doesn't seem to be the same risk of offence with those. And for some reason that I can't quite get my head around, everyone seems to laugh at a bad French accent. (Except, presumably, the French! Who knows? Maybe they get their laughs from bad English accents!) Anyway, try to be sensitive; the bottom line is that it's tough to build a good storytelling relationship with an audience you've already offended.

As with faces and postures, it's important that you find a voice that's appropriate to your character. Sometimes it can be fun to work against type. A giant with a little squeaky voice can be funnier than one with a big loud voice, for example. What you don't want to do, though, is to work against the problem in your story. If the giant is meant to be evil, it's probably best not to make him funny (unless you're going for a camp kind of evil). Or if you have a character who is meant to have something quite sombre to say in the story, it might be better not to give him or her a silly voice. All you will get then are laughs when you are trying to be serious. This can be a particular problem in biblical storytelling when it comes to choosing a voice for God or for Jesus. I always go for some variation of my "normal" voice for Jesus, and I work hard to erase any trace of that breathless, pious, "religious" tone (particularly since Jesus spent a lot of his time fighting against that very thing!). As far as the voice of God goes, the temptation is always to turn up the reverb and do the deep and boomy voice. I think that works sometimes, but that it's also helpful to remember that, as in the Old Testament story of the prophet Elijah, God sometimes speaks in a "still, small voice" as well!

Aunt Mabel's Table
(from the original *Anyone Can Tell a Story*)

As mentioned earlier, this story is in this book because it's a good example of how different voices can be used to bring characters to life.

Telling tips: *Simply follow the suggestions for the voices and characters from earlier in this chapter. I don't usually include any participation, but I do pretend to pick up the tins, look at the tops and bottoms, shake them, and pretend to open them up with a pretend can opener (not a pretend electric can opener, by the way – a pretend manual one!).*

There were five cans on Aunt Mabel's table.
    One for Aunt Mabel.
    One for my oldest cousin, Sue.
    One for my Uncle Joe.
    One for my older cousin, Tom.
    And one for me, Alexander.

There were five cans on Aunt Mabel's table.
    And not one of them had a label!
    "I got them on sale at the supermarket!" beamed my Aunt Mabel.
    "This is like a game we play," whispered my cousin Sue.
    "You have to eat whatever is in your can," shuddered my Uncle Joe.
    "I got dog food, last time!" snickered my cousin Tom.
    I want to go home, I thought. And then I remembered what my mother told me.
    "Your Aunt Mabel is different from other people. Just try to be polite."

There were five cans on Aunt Mabel's table. So my Aunt Mabel picked up the biggest one. She looked at its top. She looked at its bottom. She looked all around the outside. Then she held it to her ear and shook it. Everybody listened.
    "Sounds like sweet, juicy peaches," guessed my Aunt Mabel.

"Sounds like round red tomatoes," guessed my cousin Sue.

"Sounds like those little white potatoes you always buy!" moaned my Uncle Joe. "The kind that make me sneeze! Cachoo!"

"Sounds like dog food," grinned my cousin Tom.

"I don't know," I said. "It just sounds all splashy and splooshy to me."

My Aunt Mabel marched the can to the counter. She fished a can opener out of a crowded drawer. And in a flash, she cranked off the lid.

"Look!" she cried. "Look! It's peaches! I love peaches! Who's next?"

There were four cans on Aunt Mabel's table. So my oldest cousin, Sue, picked up the smallest can. She looked at its top. She looked at its bottom. She looked all around the outside. Then she held it to her ear and shook it. Everybody listened.

"Sounds like soft flaky tuna!" guessed my Aunt Mabel.

"Or thick pink salmon," hoped my cousin Sue.

"No! No! It sounds like that lumpy meat spread you always buy!" moaned my Uncle Joe. "The kind that makes me BURP!"

"Sounds like dog food," whispered my cousin Tom.

"I don't know," I said. "It just sounds all soft and mushy to me."

My cousin Sue took the can to the counter and she carefully opened it. But when she turned around with the can between her hands, there was this disgusted look on her face.

"It's spinach!" she groaned. "I hate spinach! Who's next?"

There were three cans on Aunt Mabel's table. And they were all about the same size now. So my Uncle Joe cringed and picked up the one in the middle. He looked at its top. He looked at its bottom. He looked all around the outside. Then he held it to his ear and shook it. Everybody listened.

"Sounds like pears in thick syrup," guessed my Aunt Mabel.

"Sounds like creamed corn," guessed my cousin Sue.

"No! No! It sounds like those kidney beans you always buy!" moaned my Uncle Joe. "The kind that make me itch!"

"Sounds like dog food," sneered my cousin Tom.

"I don't know!" I said. "It sounds like... it sounds like... it sounds like... peas!" I was trying to be polite.

My Uncle Joe took the can to the counter and he opened it. But when he turned around with the can between his hands, there was an even more disgusted look on his face.

"It's kidney beans!" he moaned. "I'm itching already! Who's next?"

There were two cans on Aunt Mabel's table. So my older cousin Tom picked up the one without the dent. He looked at its top. He looked at its bottom. He looked all around the outside. Then he held it to his ear and shook it. Everybody listened.

"Sounds like condensed soup," guessed my Aunt Mabel.

"Sounds like cranberry sauce," guessed my cousin Sue.

"No! No! It sounds like those pork and beans you always buy!" moaned my Uncle Joe. "The kind that make me..."

"No way, it's dog food!" interrupted my cousin Tom.

"Sounds like spaghetti!" I guessed. I was definitely catching on!

My cousin Tom took the can to the counter and opened it. But before he could turn around, I stuck my head over his shoulder and peeked.

"Look!" I shouted. "I was right! It's spaghetti!"

"But... but... I hate spaghetti!" moaned my cousin Tom. "I hate spaghetti even worse than dog food! Who's next?"

There was one can left on Aunt Mabel's table. And if I was going to be polite, I would have to eat whatever was in it. I looked at its top. I looked at its bottom. I looked all around its dented outside. Then I held it to my ear and shook it. It made no sound at all!

For the first time, my Aunt Mabel looked serious.

"It could very well be dog food," she guessed.

"Or cat food," guessed my cousin Sue.

"It's probably that beef and liver flavour," shuddered my Uncle Joe. "The kind that smells so bad."

"Woof! Woof!" barked my cousin Tom.

But I said nothing. I picked up the can and marched it to the counter.

I stuck the sharp end of the can opener into the top. I turned the handle ten whole times. Then I carefully pulled back the lid. What I saw was brown.

And thick.

And gooey.

It was a whole can of CHOCOLATE PUDDING!!

There were five of us sitting at Aunt Mabel's table.

Aunt Mabel stuck a big spoon into her bowl of peaches.

"Thank you for coming to dinner!" she said to me.

My cousin Sue looked at her plate of spinach and gagged.

My Uncle Joe looked at his kidney beans and started scratching.

My cousin Tom looked at his spaghetti and ran for the bathroom.

But I remembered what my mother told me.

"Thank you for having me," I said. Then I stuck a spoon into my bowl of chocolate pudding and – very politely – ate it all up.

Dinner in the Lions' Den

Here's the other story I referenced, voice-wise. Again, those different voices really do help the crowd to tell the characters apart – and they are fun to do!

Telling tips: *Practise and then use the voices suggested earlier in this chapter.*

King Darius did not want to dump Daniel in the lions' den. And Daniel certainly did not want to be dumped there. But a law was a law – even if the king had been tricked into making it. And Daniel had broken the law by praying to God when the law said he shouldn't.

So while Daniel's enemies were laughing and slapping each other on the back for tricking the king in the first place, two things happened.

King Darius sent up a prayer, like a little white bird, to ask Daniel's God to protect Daniel.

And Daniel sent up a little white bird of his own.

It didn't take long for God to send an answer back, but it must have seemed like ages to Daniel as he was being lowered into the lions' den.

There were four lions in the lions' den.

A huge father lion with a shaggy brown mane. A sleek mother lion with golden brown fur. And two tumbling lion cubs.

The lions looked at Daniel and drooled. Their tummies growled like only lion tummies can.

"He's skinny and scrawny and old," moaned Father Lion.

"He's tough," said Mother Lion. "But he'll be tasty."

"Dibs on the drumsticks!" said one of the cubs.

But all Daniel saw were four open mouths and four sets of sharp white teeth. And all Daniel heard was a rising, roaring chorus as the lions padded closer.

Suddenly, something like a curtain opened up between heaven and earth. God had heard Daniel's prayer, and God's answer had arrived! God's answer was an angel. A great big angel who was good with lions! An angel who looked a bit like a lion himself. A great, stocky slab-footed angel with hulking hands and a shaggy brown head of hair.

"Wait just a minute!" called the angel. "It's not time to eat yet."

"Oh?" growled Father Lion. "Then what time is it, Mr Angel?"

The angel paused for a moment and thought.

"It's scratching time," he said.

Then the angel laid one huge hand on Father Lion's head and started scratching behind his ears. Those chunky fingers felt good, and Father Lion stopped his growling, laid himself down and began to purr. With his other hand, the angel scratched Mother Lion at the base of her neck, where it met her shoulders. Soon, she was purring, too.

"Me next! Me next!" shouted the cubs. And for a long time, Daniel heard nothing but scratching and purring and mewing.

Then one of the lion's tummies started to growl again. Father Lion glared at Daniel through his mane and rolled a pink tongue across his lips and showed the end of one long white fang.

"What time is it now, Mr Angel?" he asked.

"It's belly-rubbing time, of course!" answered the angel.

Father Lion muttered a disappointed "Oh", but the other members of his family were quite excited.

"Me first!" mewed one of the cubs.

"You were first the last time," mewed the other.

"There'll be turns for everyone," said the angel as he turned over a cub with each hand. Then he smiled at Daniel and winked.

And then... you know how it is with belly rubbing. First you're rubbing bellies and then you're wrestling. If any of Daniel's enemies had found the courage to put his ear to the stone on top of the den, he would have thought that old Daniel was being torn to pieces. But it was only the lions rolling and biting and pawing at each other as they played "Trap the Tail" and "Cuff the Cub". And that great, tawny angel was playing hardest of all.

When they had finished, the lions collapsed, exhausted, on the floor of their den.

"What time is it? What time is it now, Mr Angel?" yawned Father Lion.

The angel stretched wide his arms, shook his shaggy head and yawned back, "It's sleeping time."

And the lions curled up like house cats in front of a fire and were soon fast asleep. The angel curled up with them, wrapping his long, lion-like self around them. But he kept one eye open, just in case.

The next morning everyone in the den was awakened by the crunching, scraping sound of the stone den's cover being hastily slid aside.

"Daniel!" the king's voice echoed through the den. "Daniel! Has your God answered my prayer? Has your God saved you?"

"Yes, Your Majesty, he has indeed," Daniel's sleepy voice bounced back up into the light. "God has answered both our prayers. He sent his angel to shut the lions' mouths."

The delighted king had his servants quickly pull Daniel out of the den. Then they dropped Daniel's enemies – those laughing, backslapping tricksters – into the den instead.

The lions stretched and stood up and stared. They were wide awake now. And very hungry.

The angel stretched and stood up too. "Well, I must go now," he said.

"Goodbye, lions."

And then he pulled back that mysterious curtain between heaven and earth and started to step inside.

"Wait!" growled Father Lion. "Before you go... tell me, what time is it now, Mr Angel?"

The angel looked at Daniel's enemies and the four hungry lions. And he grinned a wide cat grin. Then he drew the curtain around him, leaving only his answer and a shadow of that grin behind.

"What time is it?" said the angel. "It's dinner time!"

Repetition

Here's a little quiz! When you think of the story of the Three Little Pigs, what phrase comes to mind? "I'll huff and I'll puff and I'll blow your house down"? Or maybe "Little Pig, Little Pig, let me come in" and "Not by the hair of my chinny-chin-chin". And how about the phrase that you connect with the Three Bears? "Who's been sleeping in my bed?" right? And Jack and the Beanstalk? "Fee-Fi-Fo-Fum, I smell the blood of an Englishman!" Of course!

And what is the reason that you remember those phrases? It's because they are repeated, over and over again throughout those much-loved stories.

My grandson, Malachi, is only four. But when I say "Little Pig, Little Pig, let me come in!", he knows exactly how to respond. Because repetition works! It's a very important part of traditional storytelling. And here's why.

First of all, repetition helps the storyteller to remember the story! Once upon a time, stories were not written down. They were passed on, orally, from teller to teller. Repetitive devices helped to keep the story anchored in the teller's head. That's why repetition often takes place at the transition points in stories – to conclude one section or set up another. It saves the teller from having to think about how to get into the next part. It's there, in the mind, as a kind of breathing space.

Similarly, repetition also helps to make the story more memorable for the audience. Tim and I would go back to the same schools, year after year, and invariably we would be greeted by kids shouting out a repetitive phrase from the year before (and sometimes even four or five years before). The phrases stuck – and so did the story along with them.

Repetition also helps to build tension in a story. The audience soon catches on to the fact that certain phrases or actions will happen again and again. Then they look forward to the repetition, expect it, anticipate it, and enjoy it when it comes round again. So if that repetitive device is linked to the problem in some way (as it often is), then it serves to create the kind of tension that every story needs on its way to a resolution.

Finally, repetition encourages participation. There is a wonderful Puerto Rican tale about a grandmother struggling to put her grandson to bed. The bedroom door is squeaky and every time she shuts it, it wakes him up. So she fills his bed with a variety of pets to keep him company. The sounds of the door and the boy and the animals are repeated over and over again. And I find that I don't even have to tell the audience to make those sounds along with me. After I have repeated them a time or two, they catch on to how the story works and jump right in. That kind of spontaneous participation is a wonderful thing, but it happens in that particular story only because of the repetition.

What this story also demonstrates is that repetition is particularly effective with younger children. I think it has something to do with the confidence that comes from catching on to the pattern of the story. It's similar, in a way, to what happens in the television series, *Teletubbies*. There is that moment, in every episode, where the audience sees a short film on one of the Teletubbies' bellies. And when the film is over, what do all the Teletubbies say? That's right, "Again, again!" Yes, that bit is repetitive as well – but that's not the bit I'm referring to. Adults don't need to see that short film again. And most of them don't want to. But for the target audience, seeing the film again is just the right thing. Because the second time round, they've got it! There are no surprises. Nothing to be scared by, if you are so inclined. They know what's going to happen. They have caught on. They get it! And in a world where there's lots they don't yet get, that inspires a certain amount of confidence and security and they can enjoy it even more the second time.

So when I retell stories for very young children, I make sure that I include lots of repetition. Because they like it *and* they need it.

I still include repetition for older audiences (for all the reasons I have stated above) and because even adults enjoy a bit of repetition. You see it when you hear your favourite song, and the guitarist hits that chord to kick off the chorus, and you start singing along!

Some of the stories that you tell will already have those repetitive devices built into them and I encourage you to use them. But if those devices are not there already, it's not that hard to come up with repetition of your own. Once again, keep it simple – a phrase, a response, an action (something that's easy to catch on to and fun to do) will keep your audience with you, right through to the end.

At the end of this section, you will find a number of retellings that depend totally on repetition – stories that are simply a series of "verses" (only this isn't poetry), each comprising two repeated lines. There are two reasons why I wrote them this way. The first is that they "work". Repeating the first line three times gives the teller the opportunity to milk the maximum meaning out of the line – to emphasize one part of the sentence the first time it is said and different parts on the subsequent times.

I always teach all the actions at the start – because it's fun and it sets the mood for the story. But I know, just as the audience does, that without a bit of prompting along the way through the story, they won't remember what those actions are. Doing the second line three times, first reminds them of the action and then gives them the chance to catch up with and enjoy what they have been given to do.

That's the "official" reason for structuring the stories in that way. The "historical" reason is that I was once given a nine-minute slot to tell a story, but only had three minutes'-worth of material in the piece – so I figured that if I just did everything three times... well, you do the maths!

There Once Lived a Man

This is one of those "three repeated line" stories I've just described. Here's how to tell it.

Telling tips: *The first three lines in each "verse" are yours to say. I always try to say the line a little differently each time, to keep it interesting. The second three lines are for your group, who also have an action to perform (described in parentheses at the end of the verse). Lead your group in that action each of the three times they say that second line. You will need to start the story by teaching all the actions. It's fun, and it also piques their curiosity – what will this story be about?*

> There once lived a man in a place called Decapolis.
> There once lived a man in a place called Decapolis.
> There once lived a man in a place called Decapolis.
> He could hardly speak. And he couldn't hear.
> He could hardly speak. And he couldn't hear.
> He could hardly speak. And he couldn't hear.
> *(Action – hold hand to ear, as if hard of hearing)*
>
> So when Jesus came visiting, his friends had an idea,
> So when Jesus came visiting, his friends had an idea,
> So when Jesus came visiting, his friends had an idea,
> And they took him by the hand and brought him near.
> And they took him by the hand and brought him near.
> And they took him by the hand and brought him near.
> *(Action – reach out arm and pretend to pull someone close to you)*
>
> "Touch our friend," they begged. "And please make him well."
> "Touch our friend," they begged. "And please make him well."
> "Touch our friend," they begged. "And please make him well."
> "You're a healer," they say. "Without peer!"
> "You're a healer," they say. "Without peer!"
> "You're a healer," they say. "Without peer!"
> *(Action – pretend to knight someone)*

So Jesus put a hand on each side of the deaf man's head.
So Jesus put a hand on each side of the deaf man's head.
So Jesus put a hand on each side of the deaf man's head.
Then stuck a finger into each ear.
Then stuck a finger into each ear.
Then stuck a finger into each ear.
(Action – put a finger in each of your ears.)

Then he spat on one finger and touched the deaf man's tongue.
Then he spat on one finger and touched the deaf man's tongue.
Then he spat on one finger and touched the deaf man's tongue.
Unexpectedly expectorating here!
Unexpectedly expectorating here!
Unexpectedly expectorating here!
(Action – point to own tongue.)

Then he looked up to heaven and sighed the word "Ephphatha".
Then he looked up to heaven and sighed the word "Ephphatha".
Then he looked up to heaven and sighed the word "Ephphatha".
Which means "Open up. Make the blockage disappear."
Which means "Open up. Make the blockage disappear."
Which means "Open up. Make the blockage disappear."
(Action – wave hands in front of face like a magician)

And the man's ears were opened. And his mouth was opened too.
And the man's ears were opened. And his mouth was opened too.
And the man's ears were opened. And his mouth was opened too.
And everything he said was plain and clear.
And everything he said was plain and clear.
And everything he said was plain and clear.
(Action – act as if you are cleaning a window.)

The people who saw it were simply amazed.
The people who saw it were simply amazed.
The people who saw it were simply amazed.

Filled with wonder. Filled with awe. Filled with fear.
Filled with wonder. Filled with awe. Filled with fear.
Filled with wonder. Filled with awe. Filled with fear.
(Action – tremble with fear/pretend to bite nails.)

So the man who couldn't speak spoke to everyone about Jesus.
So the man who couldn't speak spoke to everyone about Jesus.
So the man who couldn't speak spoke to everyone about Jesus.
And they heard the word from the man who couldn't hear.
And they heard the word from the man who couldn't hear.
And they heard the word from the man who couldn't hear.
(Action – repeat action from verse one)

A Wife for Isaac

I love "counting" stories! And kids seem to like them, too. So the repetition built into this story is a counting kind of repetition. The counting serves to break the story up into sections and effectively announces transitions in the narrative. But it also serves to remind the hearer of the main problem.

Telling tips: *Break your group up into three sections. Teach the first section: "Ten Camels, Nine Camels, Camel Number Eight". Teach the second section: "Seven Camels, Six Camels, Five Camels, Four". And then last section: "Three Camels, Two Camels, Camel Number One". Don't teach them the last line in each of their sections, mainly because one of those lines changes at the end and you will need to say that. So, for example, let them do the counting in each section, "Ten Camels, Nine Camels, Camel Number Eight", and then you finish off with the final line – "He waited at the well outside the city gate."*

Ten Camels
Nine Camels
Camel Number Eight
He waited at the well outside the city gate.

Seven Camels
Six Camels
Five Camels
Four
The servant waited at the city of Nahor.

Three Camels
Two Camels
Camel Number One
He was looking for a wife for his master's son.

Abraham could not have been more clear:

"I do not want my son Isaac to marry a Caananite girl. So go to the land I came from, to the city of Nahor, and find a wife for him there. Then bring her back here.

"Do not take my son with you, or let him go to fetch his bride. He needs to stay here, in the land that God has promised us.

"You must bring her back for him."

Ten Camels
Nine Camels
Camel Number Eight
He waited at the well outside the city gate.

Seven Camels
Six Camels
Five Camels
Four
The servant waited at the city of Nahor.

Three Camels
Two Camels
Camel Number One
He was looking for a wife for his master's son.

The task seemed impossible! Who should he choose? How would he know? And how could he persuade her family to let her return with him?

"An angel." That's what his master had said. "God will send an angel ahead to prepare the way."

But as far as he could tell, there wasn't an angel in sight. Just a well. And his ten camels. And a parade of beautiful potential wives.

Ten Camels
Nine Camels
Camel Number Eight
He waited at the well outside the city gate.

Seven Camels
Six Camels
Five Camels
Four
The servant waited at the city of Nahor.

Three Camels
Two Camels
Camel Number One
He was looking for a wife for his master's son.

So the servant prayed:

"God of my master Abraham, help me. Use me to fulfil the promise you made to my master, when you said that his descendants would fill the land where you led him. Show me the woman you have chosen to wed his son."

And then he paused. And then he continued:

"Here's what I'm going to do. I'm going to ask each woman for a drink from her water jar. And if one of them offers to give water to my camels, as well, I will know that she's the one!"

Ten Camels
Nine Camels
Camel Number Eight
He waited near the well outside the city gate.

Seven Camels
Six Camels
Five Camels
Four
The servant waited at the city of Nahor.

Three Camels
Two Camels
Camel Number One
He was looking for a wife for his master's son.

Before the servant had even finished praying, a beautiful young woman called Rebecca arrived with a water jar.

She went to the well. She filled her jar. And the servant ran after her and asked her for a drink.

"Of course," she said. And when he had drunk his fill, she asked, "Can I bring some water for your camels too?"

And at once he knew. She was the one!

Ten Camels
Nine Camels
Camel Number Eight
He waited at the well outside the city gate.

Seven Camels
Six Camels
Five Camels
Four
The servant waited at the city of Nahor.

Three Camels
Two Camels
Camel Number One
He was looking for a wife for his master's son.

So, as he prayed a little prayer of thanks, the servant produced two gold bracelets and a gold nose ring and gave them to the girl. He asked her to take him (and his ten camels) to her father's house, where he told them all about his master and his mission and his hopes that she would marry his master's son.

More gifts were given – to Rebecca and to her family, too. And finally she agreed to go with the servant and meet Isaac.

So off they went – the bride-to-be, the servant, and the ten camels – to meet his master's son.

Ten Camels
Nine Camels
Camel Number Eight
He waited at the well outside the city gate.

Seven Camels
Six Camels
Five Camels
Four
The servant waited at the city of Nahor.

Three Camels
Two Camels
Camel Number One
The servant found a wife for his master's son.

Voices

Again, the simple repetitive device of just saying the word "voices" ties the story together and also moves it along. It's really exciting when you find this in a story and when you also find a way to use it.

Telling tips: *Every time you say "voices" at the start of each section, point to the crowd and have them make a "crowd noise". You can use the repeated "rhubarb" thing if you like. But don't get too silly, as the story itself is actually pretty serious.*

There were voices. More than he could count. Voices in his head. And they never stopped shouting at him or telling him what to do.

"Break the chains around your arms!"

"Tear the shackles from your legs!"

"Take that stone – the sharp one – and cut yourself. Do it! Do it now!"

"Now run! Run so far that no one will ever find you!"

He did what they told him. He always did. And that's how he came to live among the tombs at the side of the sea of Galilee.

There were voices. Men climbing out of a fishing boat. Laughing and joking at the water's edge. He tried to hide, but someone spotted him. And walked towards him. And spoke to him. In a voice so strange that all he could do was fall to his bruised knees.

"Come out of this man, evil spirit," the voice said.

There were voices – more voices – all the voices – shouting their reply. And his own voice the loudest among them.

"What do you want with me, Jesus, Son of God? Don't torture me, please!"

"What's your name?" asked the voice. Calmly. Quietly. Almost gently.

And the voices cried back, "Legion! For we are many!"

There were voices. All shut up inside him again. Telling him what to do.

"Turn your head."

"Point to the hillside. That's right, the one where the pigs are feeding."

"Now say it. Say it like you mean it."

So he did. And the words that came out were:

"Send us among the pigs."

So Jesus did. The evil spirits fled into the herd and the pigs raced down the hill into the sea, where they drowned.

There were voices. The men who were tending the pigs. The people from the town nearby. Everyone was shouting at once.

"It's like the pigs went crazy!"

"We're not sure what happened."

"But this man, here, this stranger from the boat – he was pointing at them. He said something, I'm sure."

"It's his fault. He killed our pigs!"

There were voices. But not one of them was inside his head. Not one of them was coming from him. He just sat there, silent. And then somebody noticed.

"Look, it's the madman. He's calm. He's quiet. He's still."

And then everyone else went quiet too. And they looked at Jesus. And they were afraid. Afraid of his power. Afraid of what they did not understand. And so, like the demons did, they begged him to go away.

There were voices. The voices of the crowd, confused and frightened, fading as they went. And the voices of Jesus and his friends, clambering back into their fishing boat. And finally there was his voice too. His own voice.

"Let me come with you," he begged.

But Jesus just shook his head. "No," he said. "I have something more important for you to do. Stay here. Tell your family what God has done for you today. Explain how he showed you his mercy.

"Stay. Stay here, and be my voice."

See!

This one works much like the previous story, only more subtly. "See" and other words relating to sight tie this story together.

Telling tips: *You might want to ask the crowd to do something quite simple, like shading their eyes and looking, every time you point to them. You might not want to do every "seeing" word (it could get old), but choose a few – well dispersed throughout the story.*

The King of Aram went to war against God's people. He set up his camp, intent on surprising them.

But the surprise was on him, for God showed his prophet, Elisha, exactly where the Arameans were camped, and he warned the King of Israel.

"See!" said Elisha. "The King of Aram is camped here. You might want to avoid that spot."

And when the Arameans moved, God showed him again.

"See!" said Elijah. "The King of Aram has moved his army over here now."

Time after time this happened, and the King of Aram was furious.

"There is a spy in our camp!" he shouted at his commanders. "Who is it? Tell me now!"

"There is no spy," said one of his officers. "Elisha the prophet is to blame. Somehow, he sees everything we do."

"Then find him!" roared the king. "And when you do, bring him to me. See to it. Now!"

So spies were sent to look for Elisha, and when they found him, in Dothan, an army followed and surrounded the city by night.

When Elisha's servant woke the next morning and looked out of the window, he ran to his master in a panic.

"Come and see!" he cried. "The army of Aram has us surrounded. Horses and chariots and soldiers, more than I can count."

The prophet looked as well. But he saw something else.

"Don't be afraid," he said to his servant. "Those who are with us are more than those who are with them."

The servant looked again and shook his head. "What do you mean?" he cried. "I see an army outside the city walls and not one soldier within. 'We're helpless. We're doomed."

So Elisha prayed.

"Open his eyes, Lord, so he sees what I see."

And when the servant looked again, he began to tremble, not out of fear but for wonder and joy.

"Tell me what you see," said Elisha.

"Horses," whispered the servant. "Thousands of them, all over the hills. Horses. And chariots of fire!"

"See," grinned Elisha. "It is just as I said. God is with us. And not a moment too soon, for here come the Arameans."

At that moment, the army attacked. And Elisha prayed again.

"Blind them, Lord," he prayed, "so they cannot find me."

And so God did.

"We can't see! We can't see!" cried the soldiers, stumbling into one another and falling from their chariots.

So Elisha offered to help them.

"You're looking for the prophet, aren't you?" he asked them.

"Yes! Yes!" they answered. "But we can't see! How can we possibly find him now?"

"I know where he is," said Elisha, and it was all he could do not to laugh. "Follow my voice, and I'll lead you to him."

So climbing down from their chariot and picking their way slowly along the road, the soldiers followed Elisha, listening for his voice.

And Elisha led them straight to Samaria, the capital of Israel, and into the presence of his king.

And then the prophet prayed again.

"Open their eyes, Lord, so they can see."

And when they looked. And when they saw. They were surrounded by the army of Israel!

The king of Israel was delighted!

"Shall I kill them?" he asked the prophet.

"Kill them?" cried Elisha. "Of course not. Don't you see? If you treat them well, they will go back to their master with news of your mercy and of the power of God. And perhaps that will put an end this war."

And so it did. The King of Israel prepared a feast for his prisoners, and then set them free. And when they told their story to the King of Aram, the fighting stopped.

"I don't believe it!" said the prophet's servant.

"It worked!" said the prophet's king.

And the prophet just grinned and said, "See!"

Water and Fire and Sky

Again, the repetition in this story is meant to summarize the story as a whole, in a sense, by focusing on the chief elements in the setting.

Telling tips: *Break your group into three sections. One for water – they could say the word when you point at them, and perhaps make a wavy motion with their hands. Do the same for fire, but a flame-like motion. And maybe looking up into the sky for the last group.*

Water and Fire and Sky.

The days of Elijah were coming to an end. So he chose a successor from the school of the prophets.

And the prophet's name was Elisha.

Water and Fire and Sky.

"God wants me to go to Bethel," said Elijah to Elisha. "Stay here."

"I'm coming with you," said Elisha to Elijah

"I will not leave you on your own."

Water and Fire and Sky.

So Elisha followed Elijah to Bethel.

And when he got there, the other prophets said to him, "The Lord is going to take your master today."

"I know," said Elisha. "But I'd rather not talk about it."

Water and Fire and Sky.

"Now God wants me to go to Jericho," said Elijah. "Stay here."

"No, I'm coming with you," said Elisha again.

"I will not leave you on your own."

Water and Fire and Sky.

So Elisha followed Elijah to Jericho.

And when he got there, the other prophets said to him, "The Lord is going to take your master today."

"I know," Elisha nodded. "But I'd rather not talk about it."

Water and Fire and Sky.

"The Lord has sent me to Jordan," said Elijah, at last. "Stay here."

Elisha shook his head. "I'm coming. You know that.

"I will not leave you on your own."

Water and Fire and Sky.

So Elisha followed Elijah to the River Jordan.

Fifty prophets stood and watched as Elijah took off his cloak and rolled it up and touched the water with it.

Fifty prophets stood and watched as the river parted from right to left, parted right down the middle!

Water and Fire and Sky.

Elisha followed Elijah across the river. Followed him on dry ground.

And when they got to other side, Elijah said, "The Lord is taking me today. What can I do for you before I go?"

Water and Fire and Sky.

Elisha said to Elijah, "Give me a double portion of your spirit – the power that God has given you."

"That's a hard one," said Elijah. "But I'll tell you what, if you see me when I go, you can have what your heart desires."

Water and Fire and Sky.

And all of a sudden, there was fire. Horses of fire! A chariot of fire! And as Elisha watched, Elijah was carried off by the chariot in a whirlwind up to heaven. And only his cloak was left behind.

Water and Fire and Sky.

Elisha looked into the sky. His master was gone. So he tore his clothes in grief and then picked up his master's cloak and walked back slowly to the river.

Water and Fire and Sky.

When he got to the river, the cloak in his hands, he asked a simple question: "Where now is the God of Elijah?"

And when he struck the water with the cloak, just as he'd seen his master do, he had his answer.

For the river parted again, just as it had before, and Elisha walked across on dry ground.

Water and Fire and Sky.

When he returned, the fifty prophets were waiting, amazed.

"The spirit of Elijah now rests on Elisha," they proclaimed. And they bowed before him.

"There are fifty of us," said the prophets. "Let us go and search for Elijah. Perhaps the Lord has set him down again on a mountain somewhere."

Water and Fire and Sky.

But Elisha knew better.

"No," he said. "There's no point."

But they persisted, and although they looked for three days, they found nothing.

"I told you not to go."

Eutychus Yawned

The repeated yawning ties the story together, while the additional yawning moves the story along each time and hints at how things might turn out. Again, it's really simple, but I think that simple is almost always best.

Telling tips: *Get everyone to yawn along with you. And give them a real one, if you can – or at least a really good pretend one. It will pull them into the story and get them into the mood.*

You might also want to lay your head in your hands and give a little snore at the end. Who knows? Everyone else might join you!

Eutychus yawned.

It had been a long day.

He'd risen early and done his chores,

Then run himself ragged playing with his mates.

But now it was late, really late.

Eutychus yawned and yawned.

It's not that he was bored.

It was Paul, after all, who was talking.

Paul, who had persecuted the followers of Jesus.

Paul, who had met Jesus, himself, in a blinding vision on the road – and had come to follow him too.

Paul, who had travelled the world telling everyone about Jesus' life and death and resurrection, and doing miracles in his name.

It was Paul who was talking. But he'd been talking for a long time – and it was nearly midnight.

Eutychus yawned and yawned and yawned.

The smoke from the lamps didn't help.

It burned his eyes and made him drowsy.

So he climbed onto the wide sill of an open window, perched three storeys above the street below, to get a little air.

And still Paul kept talking.

Eutychus yawned and yawned and yawned and yawned.

And then he stopped yawning.

And started snoring.

And sleeping, he slumped and then slipped off the sill and fell out the window to the ground below.

People screamed.

Paul stopped talking.

And everyone raced down the three flights of stairs to the street.

"He's dead!" someone shouted.

But Paul scooped him up in his arms and said different.

"Don't be alarmed," he cried. "The boy's alive."

And so he was!

Some of the people went back upstairs and Paul carried on with his talk. He didn't finish until daybreak!

And the rest of the people?

They took Eutychus home.

And made sure he got to bed.

"You're lucky to be alive," they said. "It's a good thing Paul was there."

And Eutychus nodded.

And Eutycus smiled.

And Eutychus yawned.

And yawned.

And yawned.

And yawned.

And yawned.

Then fell safely back to sleep.

Hand

You can see, by now, I'm sure, how a single word can pull a story together.

Telling tips: *When you say "hand", have everyone hold out a hand, or look at their hand, or maybe even hold a hand.*

Hand.

The man had a paralysed hand.

He was sitting there, in the synagogue, on the sabbath.

And Jesus was standing at the front.

Hand.

The man had a paralysed hand.

So Jesus called him forward.

And then he asked the crowd a question.

"Do you think it's right to heal this man?

"On the one hand, our Law says it's wrong to work on the sabbath day. And healing is most definitely work.

"On the other hand, it's surely right to give help when it's needed. To save a life when we can."

Hand.

The man had a paralysed hand.

But nobody in that crowd had an answer. Not one.

The Law was more important to them. More important than the man.

And that made Jesus angry.

You gotta hand it to him, though. He didn't lose his temper. He just did what he thought was right.

Hand.

The man had a paralysed hand.

"Stretch out your hand," said Jesus. And when the man did, it was paralysed no more!

Hand.

The man no longer had a paralysed hand.

And now some other people were angry.

"This is getting out of hand!" grumbled the religious leaders amongst themselves.

"It's time we did away with this Jesus," muttered one of them (and it was no off-hand remark).

So they left and they plotted and they planned.

And the man wiggled his fingers.

And tousled his children's hair.

And gripped Jesus by the shoulders and thanked him.

Hand.

The man with the paralysed hand.

Participation

Now to what is, in my opinion, the most important storytelling device of them all. If storytelling is truly a dialogue, then someone needs to get the conversation started. If storytelling is really just a verbal form of play, then it's no fun to play alone. Participation is the icebreaker that starts the conversation, the invitation for everyone to get down on their hands and knees and play.

Participation comes in many forms. At its simplest, a participation device is something that everyone in the group does together. Maybe it's an action that everyone does on cue. Maybe it's a line that everyone echoes back to the storyteller. Maybe it's a response that everyone makes when a certain word is spoken. Sometimes it's helpful to start the story by telling the crowd what they need to do at a certain point. And sometimes it works just as well to ask them to do it when you get there. The important thing, though, is that the participation device should be easy to catch on to (that simple thing again!), and fun to do.

A participation activity that's too difficult is a bit like that part of the wedding ceremony where the bride and groom have to say their vows, and the vicar gives them those long wordy chunks to repeat. Everyone feels bad when the couple stumble and fumble and mispronounce the words. And the same thing can happen in a story.

But it can be just as bad when the participation activity is simply not interesting. There's nothing better than being involved in a story where everyone is doing something together that's fun. And there's nothing worse than going through the motions to get through an activity that's not.

So how do you tell the difference? Well, you have your own experience to start with. Does a particular phrase, action, or response feel like it's fun to you? If not, then find something else. Certain things almost always work – silly noises (body noises particularly – but your repertoire really needs to extend beyond fitting raspberries somewhere into every story!), funny faces, and, for some reason, elephant and monkey impersonations. Exaggeration of any kind, in fact, will usually work – as long as you're comfortable exaggerating, yourself, and having fun with it too. That's the key, really. If you introduce an activity as if it's the best thing in the world, and the group sees that you're enjoying yourself, they are more likely to enjoy it too. And more willing to have a go in the first place.

Participation activities where everyone is doing the same thing are probably the easiest kind to initiate. There's more security for each individual if everyone looks foolish, and so you're likely to get more of the crowd involved. If some folks are not participating, however, don't harangue them. A little gentle encouragement is all right. Something like "OK, everybody now!" But singling out non-participants will not win you many friends. Some are more shy than others. Some might be struggling to do the activity or repeat the words – no matter how simple. Some might have certain disabilities, even, that make the activity more difficult for them. And some people just don't like to participate! So be gentle. Continue having fun with those who are joining in. And hope that those who aren't will catch the spirit of the thing and join in later. It's that relationship thing again. It will take longer for some folks to feel secure with you than for others. Give them time. Don't rush the relationship. And more often than not you will find them getting involved a story or two later.

A word or two about very small children, here. Many little children are frightened by loud noises. They can't stand them – they really can't. On the other hand, there are other small children who love to make loud noises! What do you do if that's one of your participation activities? You warn them, that's what. You say something like, "We're going to make a really loud noise, and if you don't like loud noises, now is the time to hold your hands over your ears!" That won't spoil things for the kids who like to make the noises. In fact, it will give them time to take a really big breath! But it will prepare the kids who don't like them. And surprisingly, it will give them the chance to make the noise too – but in a safe and secure environment. I can't tell you how many little children I've seen – hands held tight over their ears and shouting for all they're worth!

Here's another thing you might want to keep in mind, when it comes to small children and participation. I learned this the hard way, actually. When I started storytelling, I worked mainly with primary school-aged children. But then my sister, who worked in a pre-school, asked me to tell some stories to her class. When the time came for participation, I did the kind of thing I normally did with older children – I asked three of the kids to come up front and play different parts. They were simple parts and the children did very well, but just as soon as the story had finished, the other children began to shout "Again! Can we do it again?" (It was that Teletubby thing, again – see above.) You see, everybody wanted the chance to play those three parts! But in order to make that happen, I would have had to tell the story fifteen times at least! So now, when I tell stories to very small children, I give everybody the chance to do everything. And then we don't need to do everything again!

(Having said that, there is no reason that you can't repeat a story in a session, if the audience really wants you to. As a matter of fact, it happened just the other day during a story-building session with a brilliant class of Year 7s! It's the ultimate compliment, I suppose – that a group should enjoy a story so much that they want to repeat the experience.)

The final thing I need to say about participation and very small children is that they should not be put into situations where they feel too vulnerable or insecure. I was telling the story of David and Goliath, once, and chose a four-year-old girl for the part of David. Unfortunately, I left David on her own for too long, while I dealt with King Saul and Goliath. And it wasn't long before I felt someone tugging on the leg of my jeans. I looked down, and David was about to burst into tears.

"What am I supposed to do, now?" she whimpered, the panic building.

I tried to calm her down. "It's OK!" I said. "You're doing fine." But she still looked really nervous. At one time I would have simply asked her if she wanted someone else to play the part. But that can be harmful too. It wasn't her fault that I'd left her on her own for so long. So, instead, I asked her if she wanted someone else to come up and help her. As it happened, there were red-headed twin girls sitting right near the front. They were a little older than her but they were obviously her friends, so she asked if they could come up and play David too. So, suddenly, David was not one girl, but three! Not historically accurate, but it worked. As a matter of fact, it worked incredibly well! She regained her confidence, her friends supported her, and when they repeated David's lines in unison, it was brilliant!

It was that relationship thing again. The story is important, yes. You want to tell it and tell it well. But the people who participate in the story are more important, still. So if you have to stop things, or alter things, or even have a three-headed King of Israel, to make somebody feel better – then that's what you do: because participation creates possibilities that go beyond the power of the story itself.

I have seen this happen many times, but one occasion stands out in particular. It happened near the end of a storytelling session. I needed a boy to come to the front and act out a part, and I chose a little guy sitting right at the back. The teachers gasped a little when I pointed to him. (I get that a lot, actually. The cheeky attitude that can cause so much trouble in class is often perfect when it comes to picking someone to play a part. I don't know how many times that teachers have told me afterwards, "You picked the naughtiest kid in the school!") Anyway, I pointed to this child, the teachers gasped, and then he came up and did a great job. And then, during lunch, the teachers told me this boy's story. It turns out that reason they gasped was not because he was naughty, but because he was terrified of standing in front of a crowd. He had cried right through the school Christmas play, and they were worried that being up front during the story would have the same effect. Well, it didn't. And I would like to think that the secure and joyous environment that we were all a part of in that storytelling event had helped that little boy to find a way past his fears. Yes, participation is great. It makes any story better. But if it can help make somebody in the audience better, too – then that's the best thing of all!

So how do you choose a volunteer, when the participation activity requires an individual and not the whole group doing the same thing together? As I said earlier, you start by looking for that cheeky expression or that smiling face. Ideally, you want a volunteer who really wants to be in front of the crowd – someone who will enjoy the moment and help others enjoy it, too. Sometimes the crowd itself gives you a clue. One child will have her hand up and others around her will be pointing at her, as well. That's often a good choice, because the others think she's funny, or popular, and want to see her up there. This is especially true when it comes to choosing teachers as volunteers. When Tim and I did our assembly programmes, we always built a place into the story where we would need a teacher to come up to the front. Kids love to see their teachers doing silly, ridiculous things. But you have to be careful. We made sure that our teacher participation time was somewhere in the middle of the story. That gave us time to look around – to see which teachers were really enjoying themselves – because we wanted to go for someone who was a good sport. Again, the children would often make the choice for us. We'd ask for a teacher's help and all fingers would point to one man or one woman in particular. It's not that the kids wanted to see someone humiliated. They seldom knew what was coming, anyway. Instead, they knew who would be fun! They knew who made them laugh. And that's who they wanted to see up front.

What if no one volunteers? Then you do a little coaxing, have a little fun, assure the crowd that the activity won't be difficult. And if you're still stuck, you can ask two people to do one job (like our little David who needed that added security), offer to do it yourself, or just take a chance and pick someone who's been smiling all along (even if their hand's not in the air!). Sometimes you get lucky and that little extra coaxing does the trick. And then, of course, once the rest of the audience sees that the volunteers are having fun, you have much less trouble getting someone next time round!

Have I made some bad choices through the years? Sure, it's inevitable. There have been the odd occasions (some truly odd!), where volunteers have refused to do certain things, or frozen, or been so wild and over the top that it was difficult to control them. And then there was that teacher – just the one, amazingly – who told me exactly what I could do with my participation activity! But, remember, this was over a twelve-year period, in front of hundreds of thousands of people. And in most of those stories, the participation went very well indeed. Sure, using volunteers is a risk. But it's one I'd take any day, because when it works (and it usually does), it brings an element of freshness and variety and surprise into the stories that would not otherwise be there. And, as I think I have demonstrated, it has the potential to do so many positive things for the participants, themselves.

Finally, here are a few more participation "tips" you might find helpful. Always be friendly and encouraging. I like to ask the name of the person who has come to the front and shake his or her hand. It helps to make that person feel more comfortable, I think, and lets him know that he is more than a moving "prop". It also makes it easier to refer to that person by name if something unusually fun happens, or you want to remark on the "performance" in one way or another. And I do think that each "performance" should elicit some remark – a clap at the very least, a "well done", or something more, if what happened was really special. Sometimes you find that you really relate well to the volunteer, and she feels free to comment, and you do too – and a little repartee develops. That's fine, as long as the rest of the audience isn't left out – as long as it continues to serve the story. It's back to the basics again – relationships and playing. If that's what's going on up front with the volunteers, then everyone will have a better time.

The same rule applies to individuals as it does to groups – make sure that the participation is simple and interesting. If there are "lines" to repeat, break them into little chunks – make them easy. Most of the time, I just say the line, myself, at that point in the story, and then have the volunteer repeat it after me. That way, we both get to enjoy ourselves as we say it, and the volunteer doesn't have to stand there worrying about whether or not she'll get the words right. If it's an action, make it clear what you want the volunteer to do. And if there is any difficulty, put the volunteer first. Always give that person the chance to step down gracefully if he doesn't feel comfortable.

Jesus Rides a Donkey Down the Hill

I suppose I could have chosen any number of stories that I have already cited as examples of what you can do in a story with participation. But I have chosen a couple from *The Storyteller Easter Book* mainly because it is due to go out of print soon and I really like them. There aren't that many collections of Easter stories about, and I wanted to make sure that most of these continued to be available (some have found their way into the new version of *The Lion Storyteller Bible*, as well).

Telling tips: *The participation in this one is very simple. Just tell the whole group to shout "hee-haw" when you point to them, or "hooray", or grumble (as appropriate). It might work equally well with three groups, but the "grumbling" group might literally grumble, seeing as they only have one thing to do!*

"I need a donkey," said Jesus to his friends.
   "I need a donkey." *(Hee-Haw!)*
   "And if the owner of the donkey should ask you what you're doing,
   Say, 'I need to ride the donkey down the hill.
   I need to ride the donkey down the hill.'"
   So Jesus' friends went to find a donkey.
   They went to find a donkey. *(Hee-Haw!)*

And when the owner asked, they simply answered,
   "Jesus needs to ride the donkey down the hill.
   Jesus needs to ride the donkey down the hill."

Then Jesus' friends put a cloak onto the donkey.
   A cloak, not a saddle. *(Hee-Haw!)*
   Then Jesus climbed on and headed for Jerusalem.
   And Jesus rode the donkey down the hill.
   And Jesus rode the donkey down the hill.

The people were surprised when they saw him on the donkey,
   When they saw him on the donkey. *(Hee-Haw!)*

Then they remembered a promise – a promise from a prophet
About a king who rides a donkey down the hill.
About a king who rides a donkey down the hill.
So the people cheered when they saw him on the donkey.
The people cheered. *(Hooray!)*
They cried, "Hosanna! Save us, Lord!"
As Jesus rode the donkey down the hill.
As Jesus rode the donkey down the hill.

Then they laid their cloaks in front of the donkey,
And they laid down palm branches too. *(Hooray!)*
And they treated Jesus just like a king.
As Jesus rode the donkey down the hill.
As Jesus rode the donkey down the hill.

But the religious leaders grumbled and groaned.
They cursed and swore and moaned. *(Moan! Moan!)*
"You're no king!" they cried. "You're nobody special!"
As Jesus rode the donkey down the hill.
As Jesus rode the donkey down the hill.

"Say what you like!" called Jesus to the leaders.
"Be as stubborn as donkeys!" *(Hee-Haw!)*
"If these stones could speak, they'd join with the people
And cheer the one who rides the donkey down the hill.
And cheer the one who rides the donkey down the hill!"

Camels, Bugs and Dirty Bowls

Here's a slightly different way of encouraging participation. And everyone has to listen carefully if they're going to get involved.

Telling tips: *Instead of teaching the crowd what to do ahead of time, simply tell them that, throughout the story, they will hear the line, "And the people said..." followed by whatever it is that the people said. Tell them that you will say what the people said first, and that they just need to echo you. So if you say "Yuck!" they say "Yuck!" back. The key is for you to make each word or phrase as funny or powerful or interesting as you can.*

That's OK throughout most of this retelling, because Jesus is making fun of his enemies. However, I always slow it down and get serious at the end, when Jesus talks about the persecution of the prophets and his own impending death.

"Watch out for the religious leaders," Jesus warned the people. "I've said it before, and I'll say it again. Watch out for them – for they teach one thing and do another. It's all just pretend – a show. They act as if they want to please God, but they're really just trying to impress one another.

"Imagine you had a bowl of soup," said Jesus.

And the people said, "Mmm." *(Mmm.)*

"Now imagine there was a bug in the soup," said Jesus.

And the people said, "Urgh!" *(Urgh!)*

"And what if there was something else floating in the soup?" said Jesus.

And the people said, "What?" *(What?)*

"How about a camel?" said Jesus.

And the people said, "Whoa!" *(Whoa!)*

"Now you wouldn't want a bug or a camel in your soup, would you?" asked Jesus.

And the people said, "No!" *(No!)*

"But the religious leaders," said Jesus, "would go to all kinds of trouble to strain out that little bug, then quite happily swallow that camel down whole!"

And the people said, "Yuck!" *(Yuck!)*

"Exactly," said Jesus. "They pay lots of attention to all the little, bug-sized details of their religion – what to wear, how to wash, how much of each tiny herb and spice they should give away. But they pay no attention at all to the big, camel-sized things – like loving one another and taking care of the poor. So watch out for them; they'll lead you the wrong way."

Then, just as if he'd finished the soup himself, Jesus held up a bowl, so the crowd could only see the outside.

"What do you think?" asked Jesus.

And the people said, "Lovely!" *(Lovely!)*

Then he turned it around so that everyone could see the old food that was caked inside.

"What do you think of it now?" he asked.

And the people said, "Disgusting!" *(Disgusting!)*

"And so are the religious leaders," said Jesus. "They look good on the outside – all pious and prim and proper – but on the inside they are dirty with selfishness and jealousy and greed."

Finally, Jesus pointed across the hill to a cemetery.

"Can you see those bright, shiny tombs?" he asked.

And the people said, "We can!" *(We can!)*

"They look nice, don't they? But what's inside them?" asked Jesus.

And the people answered, "Dead men's bones." *(Dead men's bones.)*

"And so it is with the religious leaders," said Jesus again. "Shiny on the outside, with all their pretending, but cold and dead inside – dead to the needs of others. And dead to what pleases God as well.

"And the saddest thing of all is that they can't even see it.

"'We want to make God happy!' they say. 'We want to do what's right.' But every time God sends somebody to talk to them – to show them how to stop pretending and let God make them really alive and really good from the inside out – what do they do? They put that person to death."

Then Jesus looked at the crowd. And his look was very serious.

"Sadly," he said, "I think they mean to do that to me."

Practising the Story

I like to be on my own when I practise a story. I tell it to myself, over and over again, not so much to memorize it word by word, but to make sure that I am thoroughly familiar with it.

I pay particular attention to those places where I intend to inject a participation activity. How will I introduce it? At the start? When I get to that point in the story? And how do I avoid disrupting the flow?

I also pay a lot of attention to any repetition devices. After all, repetition only works if it's repeated! So it's very important to remember where you're planning to use these devices.

I do all of this until I feel comfortable with the story – that's the best way I can describe it. It's a sense of confidence so that I feel ready to stand in front of a crowd and at least look as if I know what I'm doing! However, no matter how much preparation I do, the fact of the matter is that with a new story, I'm never really sure how it will "work" until I try it. I have enough experience to make a good guess, but until I hear an audience laugh at what I assumed would be the funny bits, and join in with what I thought would be the participation bits, and stay dead quiet at what I hoped would be the tense, or serious, or weepy bits, I can never really be sure. That's the true test – and because I'm working in situations where I can tell the same stories over and over again, I always know I'll get another shot at it! That's reassuring, in and of itself, and an incentive to stick with a story and improve it, even if things don't work perfectly the first time. What is exciting is to watch a good story mature, grow and develop, until it works really well.

But maybe you're not in that situation. Maybe you have to tell stories to the same audience – in school, or Sunday school – week after week, and there isn't the chance to do the same story twice. The same principles apply to that situation, as well. No, you can't watch a single story develop through time – but you do have a better chance to get to know your audience, and therefore to experience some sense of development and maturity in the storytelling relationship itself. So as you learn what your regular audience thinks is funny, or sad, or interesting, you develop a sense of confidence from that, as well. And then you know when you've found a story that will really work with that particular group. In my church work, I have certainly found that to be the case when it comes to preaching to the same congregation week after week. And I think it is true of storytelling, as well.

Finally, you may well be no good at memorizing at all. Let me assure you then, that if you read a text over and over again, and find some participation activities to get the audience involved, and simply become very familiar with your story, that you can get away with using a book, as well. It's not ideal, granted. You do lose some flexibility, in terms of the use of your hands and eyes. But it can be done, and done well. And if that's what you need to feel confident, particularly at first, that's fine. But I suspect that it won't be long before you will want to put the book down!

Another thing you can do is print the story in large type that you can easily see (I'm up to 22 point now!) and put it in a binder on a stand in front of you – so your hands are both free. That way, you can glance at the text, but still keep most of your attention on the crowd. If you are preparing a new story every week, this technique can be really helpful.

I hope that this chapter has helped you to see that the right kind of preparation and practice is essential for effective storytelling. Yes, it takes time and effort, but it's well worth it in terms of the quality of the stories you tell. And what's more, it's fun! I love being in front of a group of people. But I also love that moment when a good storytelling "hook" or "device" comes to me, alone, in my study! I can't wait to try it out. And if it's a good one, then the time and the thought and the struggle are all forgotten – replaced by the satisfaction I feel when the story goes down well, and by the look on the faces of the listeners too. The look you only get when a story has been well told.

Chapter Five

Reading the Bible

You've been there and I have too.

Someone stands up to read the scripture passage for the morning service and it is obvious, immediately, that they have not looked at it beforehand. They don't know what the passage is about. And the tone of their delivery suggests they don't care, either. They get the words out – that's about it. And since much of the congregation has switched off, anyway, nobody notices or seems to care.

Or how about this? The preacher is in the middle of his sermon. He needs to read a bit of scripture to make a point, to move the sermon along. And when it comes out, it's rushed, hurried, sped through – so he can get back to what (I'm assuming he assumes) is the really important stuff – the stuff he wrote!

I don't think I'm being too hard here. And because I've preached my fair share of sermons through the years, I think I have the right and the experience to address this. When it comes to the public reading of scripture, it seems that, regardless of what we say or believe, many of us don't have much respect for God's Word. Because if we did, we'd take the time and make the effort to read it well.

Now I'm not talking for a minute about people who can't read well. That's not the problem. The problem lies with those of us who are perfectly capable, but just can't be bothered to prepare.

One of my favourite worship leaders is Geraldine Latty. Years ago, I went to a workshop she led on the subject and was particularly impressed by the way she prepared to lead worship through the songs she had chosen. She said that she meditated on the meaning of the words of the songs – let them soak into her, so she knew exactly what they were saying. Only then was she ready to use them to lead a congregation in worship. It's that kind of preparation that we need to bring to the public reading of God's Word – not the slapdash, "grab a Bible and head for the front, thumbing through for the passage along the way" approach.

"But I'm busy!" you say. And I hear you. I'm busy too. But that's not the point. If we truly believe that God has given us his Word so that we can know who he is – then reading that Word well, like telling the story well, needs to be done with care and respect and creativity and passion and understanding. It's no frivolous exercise, being asked to read God's Word. It's a responsibility with potentially eternal consequences, because God's Word is powerful, it does things, it changes people's lives. Not the spilling out of the words – like they have some magical effect just because they have landed on the ear – but the careful, considered, prepared and intelligible passing on of their content.

The reason that I have put this chapter at the end of a book on storytelling is that the basic principles that make for a good retelling of a Bible story are essentially the same as those that make for an effective public reading of the text.

Therefore, it you want to read a Bible passage well in front of other people, the first thing you need to do is to read it to yourself. Not once. Not twice. But several times, to start with. To get a feel for it – to get some initial sense as to what it is about.

The first thing you need to ask, as you read the text, is: What kind of writing is this?

Is it a story? Then you need to read it like a story – you need to know who the characters are, what the setting is, what the main problem is.

Is it a letter? Then you need to read it like a letter – particularly if it's one of those letters that is quite personal. Granted, some of Paul's letters are more like theological essays, and you need to treat them as such. But the ones that sound like letters need to be read like letters – in a personal, chatty style. I tried that at Spring Harvest, a few years ago, when the Bible readings were based on the book of Philippians. I just read it like I would have read a letter from a friend out loud. And the difference was amazing. It just made more sense to me, for a start. And I got no end of really positive comments from the guests, who felt like they had found new meaning in it too.

Is it an essay/treatise-like piece? Then you need to focus on making what is often very dense language feel simple and straightforward, breaking it up, by using pauses, into understandable chunks.

Is it a psalm? If so, what kind of psalm? You read a lament differently to a song of praise. A cry for help in a different tone than that for a cry for vengeance (and the psalms are full of those!).

Is it a list? Much prayer is needed here – not only for pronunciation's sake, but also to keep the crowd's attention. I don't think, in such cases, that it hurts to precede the reading with some kind of introduction – here's a list, here's why its in the Bible, maybe you want to listen for what you think is the strangest name!

In each case, whatever the genre, the key is for you to understand the text before you read it to someone else. Because understanding it yourself is essential to reading it in such a way that the congregation will understand it too.

"But isn't that the preacher's job?" you say. Well, to a certain extent, yes. But no preacher I know would be unhappy with a reading that kicks off her sermon so that people are already excited about the text, have some sense of its meaning, and are eager to find out more. That's got to be better than standing up in front of a crowd that has just been rendered comatose by a droning, unintelligible rehearsal of three obscure passages.

Furthermore, in churches that depend on some form of lectionary, the preacher may only deal with one of the texts that are read. So there is an even greater responsibility to read the other texts well.

You need to understand what the text is about. And if you don't get it on your own, then you need to look for some help. Ask your pastor or priest about it, for a start. And if they intend to emphasize one aspect of the text, it wouldn't hurt to know that – so you can emphasize it, as well, as you read. A good commentary helps too. Tom Wright's "For Everyone" series of commentaries on the New Testament is, in my opinion, the very best place to start. These books benefit from his years of scholarship, yet his writing style is really accessible. And his comments on most passages that you will read from the front are no more than a few pages long.

Once you understand what you will be reading, you need to ask yourself what you need to do so that your listeners will understand the passage, as well.

Sometimes, they will need to know what happened in the passage just before the bit you are reading. I read a passage at a conference just a few weeks ago that followed one of Paul's meditations on the resurrection. It was key for the group to be informed of that before I read the passage – otherwise his "and so..." made no sense. If your listeners need to know that – tell them. Don't preach a sermon, mind you (that's someone else's job!), but take thirty seconds to fill them in.

Sometimes, you will need to break up the passage into more accessible bits. You can do that, as I suggested above, by pausing. You can also do that, sometimes, by using more than one voice. Or by giving the congregation a voice.

Now, I realize that I could be on shaky ground here. In some traditions, the idea of one reader for the Old Testament, another for the Psalm, another for the Gospel is pretty well sacrosanct. Fair enough. But if there is flexibility in your church, then I think it's worth experimenting with different voices as you read the text.

Narrative texts will often benefit from the use of more than one voice, particularly if the dialogue in the text is at the heart of it. Abraham's discussion with God about the fate of Sodom and Gomorrah is a good example. Two voices could make that passage really clear.

This is also the case with some of the psalms, where a chorus or some other kind of response follows a verse. Using another voice with yours, or asking the congregation to call back the response, breaks up the reading and makes it more accessible. If you're going to involve the congregation in your reading, though, it's essential that you are all reading from the same translation. So if you have pew Bibles, use those. And if not, put the reading on your order of service or whatever kind of screen you use.

Another place where more than one voice can work is where the author of the text is contrasting one thing with another. I did a reading, recently, from 2 Corinthians 6:8–10, where Paul does this over the course of those three verses. So I had one side of the room say the first bit (through glory) and the other side say the contrasting bit back (and dishonour). It wasn't just a gimmick or a trick; it was a way of making that part of what Paul had to say more clear. That's always the goal – reading the passage so it's understood.

If you aim for that first of all, then I think you will almost always be able to make the passage more interesting. Yes, I know, it's God's Word. The congregation *should* be interested. But it's like what I said in the "finding the shine" section of the storytelling bit of this book (see chapter three): people who have been Christians for a while sometimes come to take God's Word for granted. Been there, done that, heard that. And that's especially true if they have been exposed to bad public Bible reading. They switch off. You can see it. You can feel it. So they need to be switched on again.

As I said, even just reading the passage with understanding will make for a good start. But, beyond that, there are things you can do to wake your listeners up and draw them in.

You could ask a question. Again – simple, quick, just before you start to read. You know what the passage is about, what its main themes are, where it's going. So why not say something like, "I'll be reading from X passage in the book of 2 Corinthians. Paul mentions reconciliation three times. Listen for those. See if you can figure out what he means when he uses that word."

You could sing! I'm not kidding. In Philippians, chapter 2, Paul employs what most scholars reckon were the words from an ancient hymn. So when I read that, once, I just made up a little tune, and sang those words when I got to that bit! Were people surprised? Yes (maybe it was my voice!), but it certainly caught their attention.

You could employ a bit of audience participation. Yes, I know, there is real risk here. And for further information on the subject, you might want to consult what I had to say on participation with regard to storytelling. But if it's gentle (particularly at first) and easy to do, it can help to bring the text to life.

Speaking of reconciliation reminds me of a technique I used recently, and which could be used with other key words. It was a passage from Corinthians, in fact, where Paul uses the word five or six times. Now that's a word we hear a lot in church, but again, it's so familiar that it often washes over us. So I looked up the word in the dictionary.

- *Reconcile* – what you do with accounts to get them to balance
- *Reconcile* – what you have to do to accept something you formerly disliked (as in reconciling yourself to the idea of something)
- *Reconcile* – what you do when you mend a relationship

Anyway, I took those three meanings and added the odd action/response and then broke up the congregation into three parts.

I gave the first meaning to the first group. When you hear the word reconcile and I point to you, you need to throw your hands in the air, with a surprised expression and exclaim "It's balanced!" as if you just reconciled your bank account.

The second group got the second meaning. I hate liver and onions, I told them. Many nodded in agreement. So pretend that you are holding a plate of liver and onions, I told them, look at it in disgust, say, "Liver and onions" as if you hate it, and then say, "Lovely!" as if you have been reconciled to the idea of it!

And the third group? I told them to turn to a neighbour, shout, "You're back!" and give them a great big bear hug.

Now I know what you're thinking, the author is an American, this must have happened somewhere in the midwest. No! It was in the UK – and what a huggy time we had! Honestly – there were smiles and laughter all around – as the Bible was being read! Imagine that! And best of all, we not only read about reconciliation and heard about it, we acted it out. We engaged with it – and with the meaning of the text.

Granted, if you did want to do that with a text on a Sunday morning, you might want to warn someone. It does take a bit longer to do it that way rather than to simply read the text (there is all the setting up of the responses for a start). So ask.

And don't do the same thing every time. Mix up your approaches to the text. A bit of response, a bit of action, some straight readings, because anything can become "old hat". Even a cap that is new!

So that's it, really. Telling the story. Reading the story out loud. In both cases, it starts with knowing the story and loving the story. Then passing the story on with all the creativity and passion and joy you can muster.

I hope that this book has helped you to see how you can do that. But more than that, I hope that the book has inspired you to "have a go." Because in our schools and in our communities and across our world, there are people young and old, who simply do not know the story. And they won't know it, or come to know the One the story is about, until someone tells them. And maybe, just maybe, that someone is you.

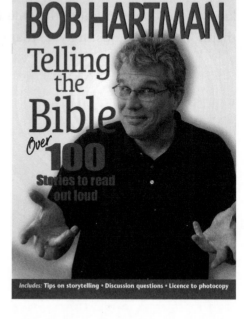

Telling the Gospel

Here are 70 powerful stories about Jesus: his birth, life, teaching, death and resurrection. Most are taken from the Gospel of Luke.

Bob uses a wide variety of narrative forms to produce stories that will delight both new Christians and Bible veterans. Each story is accompanied by an introduction which explains its particular place and function, with telling tips and special details. Each is followed by questions for discussion.

Some stories require audience participation: all are designed to entertain and inform. Some are seasonal, while others are intended for use right through the year. They can be read aloud by anyone after a little practice.

BOB HARTMAN
Telling the Gospel
70 stories about Jesus to read out loud

Includes: Tips on storytelling · Discussion questions · Licence to photocopy

"Bob Hartman is to storytelling what David Beckham is to football. An absolute master. Give him a story and no one will bend it like him."
– Pete Meadows

The book is produced in large clear print and strongly bound for durability
Includes licence to photocopy

ISBN 978-1-85424-961-6 £10.99 UK/$14.99 US

www.lionhudson.com/monarch

MONARCH